Bonus Music CD Included

The Book of
Uncommon
Prayer 2

Prayers and Worship Services
for Youth Ministry

Steven L. Case

ZONDERVAN®
GRAND RAPIDS, MICHIGAN 49530

ZONDERVAN.COM/
AUTHORTRACKER

Soul Shaper

Youth Specialties
www.youthspecialties.com

Youth Specialties

The Book of Uncommon Prayer 2: Prayers and Worship Services for Youth Ministry
Copyright © 2006 by Steven L. Case

Youth Specialties products, 300 South Pierce Street, El Cajon, CA 92020, are published by Zondervan, 5300 Patterson Avenue Southeast, Grand Rapids, MI 49530.

Library of Congress Cataloging-in-Publication Data

Case, Steve L., 1964-
   The book of uncommon prayer 2 : prayers and worship services for youth ministry / By Steven L. Case.
      p. cm.
   Includes bibliographical references and index.
   ISBN-10: 0-310-26723-4 (pbk.)
   ISBN-13: 978-0-310-26723-2 (pbk.)
   1. Youth--Prayer-books and devotions--English. I. Title.

   BV283.Y6C272 2006
   264.00835--dc22

                                                                    2006000921

Unless otherwise indicated, all Scripture quotations are taken from the Holy Bible: New International Version (North American Edition), copyright © 1973, 1978, 1984 by International Bible Society. Used by permission of Zondervan.

Web site addresses listed in this book were current at the time of publication. Please contact Youth Specialties via e-mail (YS@ YouthSpecialties.com) to report URLs that are no longer operational and provide replacement URLs if available.

Creative Team: Doug Davidson, Erika Hueneke, Rich Cairnes, and SharpSeven Design
Cover Design by SharpSeven Design

Printed in the United States

---

06 07 08 09 10 • 8 7 6 5 4 3 2 1

Contents

{ 3 }

Dedication and Acknowledgments

Dedication

The first prayers I remember hearing as a child ("Now I lay me down to sleep..." and "God is great, God is good...") were taught to me by my mother. The first church songs I remember hearing ("Jesus Loves Me" and "Tell Me the Stories of Jesus") were in her voice.

She gave me a passion for words, a love of stories, and an understanding that a sense of humor is a requirement for church work.

She never gave up on me. Ever.

This book is for my mom.

Acknowledgments

I would like to thank the good folks at Youth Specialties who said, "Yeah, we'll do another one." Especially, Doug, Jay, and Roni.

Thanks to the good folks at St. Paul's Episcopal Church in Akron, Ohio.

Thanks also to the congregation of Windermere Union Church in Windermere, Florida, who have supported every idea I've come up with.

I'd like to acknowledge Jonny Baker for his amazing music, and Holly Sharp, who "got it" when it came to understanding what this book should look like.

Special thanks to Becky, Aprille, and Eric.

More Uncommon Prayers

When I wrote *The Book of Uncommon Prayer* several years ago, it wasn't intended to be "volume 1." At the time, I never even considered the possibility of a "volume 2." But here it is.

I wrote the first collection of "uncommon" prayers because I had come to love *The Book of Common Prayer*. I'd first encountered that book in 1993, when I began working as a youth pastor for St. Paul's Episcopal Church in Akron, Ohio. Although *The Book of Common Prayer* is used every Sunday in some Christian traditions, I had never used it before starting at St. Paul's. But soon it was always with me. I used it for worship services, retreats, and lock-ins, as well as in my own personal time with my Creator.

I wrote *The Book of Uncommon Prayer* because I wanted to create a similar resource full of worship services, prayers, and responsive readings for youth workers to use. I hoped it would be a valuable tool youth pastors in all denominations could use with their groups, as well as privately.

Youth workers in both liturgical and nonliturgical traditions responded to the first book. There seemed to be something about the concept of a prayer book that appealed to everyone. No matter how gifted or talented you might be, sometimes every youth pastor needs to find a creative worship idea or a group prayer at a moment's notice. Sometimes you just need a prayer for yourself.

That's what *The Book of Uncommon Prayer* provided. And this volume offers even more worship services, prayers, and other resources to empower your work with youth.

This book is a tool for youth ministers like you who spend weeks planning the winter retreat, lining up a guest speaker, finding enough chaperones, getting some people to donate cookies, and somehow managing to drive to the retreat center without getting lost. Then you suddenly remember, "Oh no, I'm in charge of the worship service tonight."

This book will help you pray during the mission trip when your mind is too full of worries about permission slips and unsafe ladders and questions like, "Why are those two kids always standing so close to each other?" It will help you offer a prayer for healing when you have a student in the hospital and a prayer of thanks when your group climbs into the new church van for the first time. It will give you the word to offer a blessing for your youth on prom night or for the tired server who just served lunch to 20 kids in a crowded Steak n Shake on a cold Saturday in February.

{ 6 }

Inside this book, you'll find the outlines, directions, and orders of worship for nine unique and creative worship experiences. Whether you're looking to put together the kind of service that takes weeks of planning and memorizing or the kind where you just pull the van over to the rest stop and have a communion service under a Highway 61 picnic shelter, this book will help. You'll also find suggestions on using liturgical colors and the five senses in worship to enrich your worship experiences.

You'll find more than 40 short blessings and an expanded section of nearly 200 thematic prayers on a wide variety of themes. These are prayers you can use in hundreds of circumstances—prayers that will get your students involved in the process. Use these prayers and blessings on their own exactly as written, or adapt them and incorporate them into your own services.

This new volume offers an index of Scripture verses categorized by topic. You can use this index for Bible study, devotions, and planning your own worship experiences—or just use it to look cool when the rest of the committee is looking for a good "mission" verse.

Perhaps most importantly, at the end of this book you'll find a section of private prayers just for you, the youth worker. I included this series of prayers to help you connect with God in your own private prayer life. Take this book with you into your own "prayer closet" (whether that be your office, your car, a quiet spot in the woods, or the beach) and use it to talk (and listen) to your Creator.

Worship and prayer are important—they are primary ways in which we connect with God. And in the end, that is our job as youth ministers, isn't it? When you boil it down, no matter what denomination, no matter what church, no matter what theology...our job is to connect teens with God. We are here to pray and thank and praise and invoke and bless and sing and...connect.

This book is a tool for worship...

for prayer...

for leadership...

for connection.

Go connect.

The Ways of Worship

One of the problems with many worship services is that we tend to think of the congregation as the "audience." Worshipers think they are there to be entertained—and if they're not, they grow bored and disconnected. But it's important to remember that the congregation—be it one thousand people gathered in the sanctuary on Sunday morning or six teens in the back of your minivan—is not the audience. By teaching students that they are as much a part of the worship service as the choir and the pastor—and that it is *God* who is the audience (not them)—we can help them have a much more fulfilling experience.

One way to emphasize this is by making our worship services more *experiential.* We need to encourage youth to immerse themselves in worship. Let them know they can get their hands dirty with it. They can put all five senses into the experience.

Using All Five Senses in Worship

In many large congregations, the sanctuary feels more like a theater, and the worship feels a lot like a rock concert. People leave a worship service with the same "buzz" you get when you leave a show by your favorite band or performer. It's a wonderful lift. Usually, it can hold you through until the next week.

But as worship has become something you do in a stadium, we've lost something: intimacy.

Think about the worship experiences you most remember. Maybe you've had great concert experiences, but the worship experiences most of us tend to remember are the ones where fewer than 20 people were in the room. The most meaningful services in my own life have been the ones involving six people around a campfire or a small group sitting in the youth room with a guitar, a candle, and a Bible.

There's another reason campfire worship experiences work—and it's not just because we've all had too little sleep in the tent the night before. It's because we are using all five of our senses to connect to God. We smell the smoke, we hear the music and the fire, we watch the dying embers, and we feel the warmth of the flames as a cold breeze blows on our backs. We taste the bread and the wine of communion. Even standing there inhaling, we get a smoky taste in our mouths. God has given us five senses. Why do we usually use only two of them when we worship?

Let's talk about using all our senses in worship.

What Does Worship Smell Like?

Years ago I met a man who told me he had attended his first funeral—that of his grandmother—when he was about five. The funeral home in that little town was also the residence of the funeral director and his family. They lived in an upstairs apartment, and the business was downstairs. The guy I met told me that during the service, the wife of the funeral director began baking sugar cookies for the luncheon afterward. To this day, he cannot smell sugar cookies without thinking of his grandmother's funeral.

When I was in college, I worked for four years as a church custodian. It was a great gig. Part of my job was to unlock the church doors every night for evening meetings and then lock them when all the meetings were done. I could do some cleaning during the meetings and get paid for that time, or I could find a quiet office and study. (I got paid for an hour's work if all I did was lock and unlock.) If I were short on money, I'd clean the restrooms. There was a bottle of thick pink liquid I would pour into the toilet bowls after cleaning, to disinfect them. The pink stuff had a very powerful wintergreen smell. Before I started that job, I used to love wintergreen Lifesavers. But I can't eat them anymore because it makes me think of cleaning toilets. One of my students gave me a wintergreen Altoid a few years ago, and I had to spit it out.

Our sense of smell is often overlooked, yet it is one of our most powerful senses when it comes to triggering memories and imagination. What if I asked you right now to think of the smell of your grandmother's house on Thanksgiving Day, or the smell of your local coffee shop when the muffins are warm? Can you see how vivid our sense of smell is?

The Holocaust Museum uses smell very effectively on its tours. At the beginning of the tour, you can smell freshly baked bread. As the tour leads you into the camps, you begin to smell a dank, sour mold smell that is almost overpowering. The creators of the museum understood smells can be a major part of the experience.

So how can we incorporate our sense of smell into worship? Be creative!

- If you are planning a communion service, you can bake your own bread.

- If you are preaching on heaven, why not bake chocolate chip cookies?

- If you are preaching about the love of God going on forever, why not bring in evergreen branches?

- Take your kids into a damp, musty basement to talk about how the early Christians had to worship in secret or they'd be arrested and put to death.

- For a Christmas service, bring in straw to evoke the smell of a barn where the baby was laid in a manger. (Better yet, why not have the service in a barn?)

It may not always work exactly as you'd planned. (Then again, what does?) I once led a Good Friday service where we tried to create the smell of a coffin by burning cedar chips. One of my adult volunteers had a potpourri burner. She brought it in, along with something she thought would smell like cedar chips, but it actually had a vague sort of marijuana smell. It wasn't the effect we were going for, but I suppose the smell was "evocative" for some of the people who seemed to recognize it.

There is something to be said for aromatherapy. Any shopping mall will have a store with candles in hundreds of different fragrances. Think about the theme of the worship experience you are planning, and choose an appropriate fragrance.

What Does Worship Sound Like?

My grandparents used to listen to a radio worship program every Sunday morning. The show opened every week with the tolling of the "ol' church bell" calling the faithful to worship. One year, my grandparents decided they would take a vacation and travel to the church where the radio program was recorded. They were eager to worship in that congregation, and were particularly looking forward to seeing and hearing the church bell in person. But as it turned out, the "bell" was actually a guy beating on the wheel rim of a car with a hammer.

Listen to any of the old radio horror stories, and you'll find many of those stories are far more frightening than any of the movies you can see today. The reason is the imagery takes place in your mind, which is capable of imagining scenes that are much scarier than what film directors could come up with. The sound-effects men of the early days of radio were auditory artists. Orson Welles knew all about the power of sound. With a microphone and a mason jar shoved into a toilet, his 1938 radio broadcast of War of the Worlds convinced the country a spaceship was slowly opening up in Grovers Mill, New Jersey.

So what about sound in worship? Think about the sound of 30 pieces of silver jingling in a cloth bag. Think about what you might hear if you were trapped inside a whale's stomach.

One of my favorite sounds (and I have found it's a favorite sound of many other people) is the sound of rain on the roof. Few things relax me more as I read the paper on a Saturday morning on my back porch, or help me sleep better at night, than rain on the roof. But what did rain sound like to Noah and his family? Is it possible to have a volunteer spray a hose on the window of the youth room as you worship? Could that be the rain that drenched Jesus as he walked on the water?

When my youth led a Good Friday service (similar to the one on page XX), we thought the sound of a hammer hitting a nail would be a powerful reminder of the cross. As it turned out, a hammer hitting a nail didn't sound enough like a hammer hitting a nail to us, so we wound up taking two large crescent wrenches and banging them together next to a microphone.

It's not necessary to turn your worship service into a radio drama. But how much more effective would the story of Jesus' calming of the storm be if you actually heard the thunder?

What Does Worship Taste Like?

There are a lot of foods in the Bible. Here are just a few of them:

- **Milk** Exodus 3:8; Proverbs 27:27

- **Butter** Deuteronomy 32:14; 2 Samuel 17:29

- **Cheese** 1 Samuel 17:18; Job 10:10

- **Bread** 1 Samuel 17:17; Acts 20:7

- **Fish** Matthew 7:10; Luke 24:42

- **Vegetables** Proverbs 15:17; Daniel 1:12

- **Fruit** 2 Samuel 16:2; Psalm 1:3

- **Honey** Song of Solomon 5:1; Isaiah 7:15

- **Oil** Deuteronomy 12:17; Proverbs 21:17; Ezekiel 16:13

- **Vinegar** Numbers 6:3; Ruth 2:14

- **Wine** Psalm 60:3; John 2:3

Incorporating these and other tastes into worship services can bring them to life. You can even use taste to suggest other senses and feelings. Later in the book you'll find a worship service that uses Pop Rocks candy to simulate an earthquake, an Atomic FireBall to simulate the anger of God, and Sierra Mist soda to cool us down with a gentle breeze.

Think of the ways you could use tastes in your worship services. Feed your group more than just communion bread. Pass around a plate of dried fruit. Let them dip bread into honey. Elsewhere in this book you will find a Passover Seder service that is modified from the traditional Jewish service. That service uses all sorts of tastes to help make the story of the exodus more vivid—salt water for tears, bitter herbs for the difficulty of life in the desert, and so on. The Jewish people had already been using tastes and smells as part of their worship for centuries by the time Jesus was born. We as Christians are too willing to reduce our sensory experience of worship to hearing the choir, watching the minister preach (oooh, look—hand gestures!), and tasting the Wonder Bread and Welch's once a month. It's time to change that.

What Does Worship Feel Like?

This one is a little trickier. Quick—what's the largest organ on a human being? (BUZZ, I'm sorry, that's incorrect. But thanks for playing our game.) The answer is: THE SKIN.

If you're preaching about Jesus calling the fishermen, have your whole group go stand with their feet in the ocean, or in a lake, or in a kiddy pool, if that's all you have. Pass around a real fish or let them hold an actual fishing net. If you're focusing on the baptism of Jesus, find a member of your congregation with a pool and let the group wade in up to their waists. If you are preaching about the crucifixion, let them hold a sledgehammer or a railroad spike.

A number of passages in the Bible talk about God's presence as a wind or a gentle breeze. I once worked with a group of people at a Youth Specialties convention and asked how we might illustrate this. One woman suggested putting large box fans around a darkened room. Each fan's cord would lead to a contact strip behind the youth minister. At the appropriate moment, the youth minister could reach behind him and flip the switch. Suddenly half a dozen fans would spin to life, and a hurricane would materialize in the room. I've incorporated this idea into the "Elijah in the Cave" service, but it has many other possibilities as well.

I took a trip to our local Salvation Army store and bought a few soft baby blankets and some rough wool sweaters. I cut these into swatches and passed them out to my students. As we read the portion of the exodus story where the people are complaining to Moses, I had them press the itchy wool sweater fabric between their hands and rub it on their faces. Later I passed out swatches of the baby blankets and read Psalm 23.

Go stand in your closet and carefully rub your face with the sleeve of each piece of clothing you own. What feels like the shroud they wrapped our Savior in? What feels like the robes of the wise men?

Go stand in the sandbox at the nearest playground (wait till the kids are done) and feel the sand between your toes. Is this what Jesus felt on his feet as he walked the beach? Would he feel the sand for 40 days in the desert?

Your hands are meant for more than holding the hymnal and doodling on the back of the bulletin during worship. They are tools for worship.

What Does Worship Look Like?

One of the greatest ways to change the sight of your worship service is to change the site of your worship service. In other words, get out of the building!

Every day, God creates these wonderful pieces of art called sunrises and sunsets. And they change every single day! Get your group outside to worship in the evening or early morning. What kind of roof does your church have? Can you stand your group on the roof and tell them about King David pacing the roof of the palace at night?

Early churches took generations to build. The "contractor" could spend his life on one project and die long before it was over. Early churches focused much more on an "awe factor"—with high ceilings that lifted the eyes up to heaven and statues of saints in the corners. Today many churches use large screens to project visual images during a worship service. Most churchgoers are so bombarded by visual images on a daily basis that just sitting and watching the minister isn't visually stimulating enough to keep their attention.

Perhaps we need to make worship a respite from the outside world. Imagine worship as a place where you can leave behind the need to constantly stimulate the brain and just let a person "be."

Don't forget darkness is an excellent visual. Cover the windows in the room; turn out the lights so the only thing your youth can see is the candle glowing in the middle of the circle. Load them into the back of a U-Haul. Blindfold them. Take away the sense of sight and see how quickly they pay attention to what else is going on around them.

The Colors of Liturgy

As we consider what worship looks like, the topic of color deserves a special mention. Advertisers and sales persons know the power of color. Many fast food restaurants are decked out in yellows and reds because those colors tend to keep you moving. More intimate restaurants (i.e., expensive and therefore not often populated by youth ministers) tend to be painted in calming hues—earth tones and deep blues and greens. The "blue plate special" at many diners used to be a cheaper meal that was literally served on a blue plate. Since blue is generally thought a less appetizing color, diner owners felt they could serve less food on the blue plate special.

Colors also have a long and rich history in worship. The altar guild changes the colors on the pulpit and altar for a reason, you know? Using various colors to differentiate liturgical seasons became common practice in the Western church somewhere during the fourth century. In the twelfth century, Pope Innocent III established a system using five colors: violet, white, black, red, and green. Some other churches added blue and gold.

With the Reformation, these traditional uses of color were minimized in some churches. Many churches still use different colors to mark the seasons, though few know the meaning behind the colors. Colors can be used in banners, vestments, altar cloths, and tapestries. I'm told there is a church in Florida that flies flags outside of the church and changes them depending on the time of year.

Generally, the following are the accepted liturgical colors, their meanings, and the time of year during which they are most appropriately used:

RED is the color of blood and thus is used to mark Holy Week and Jesus' crucifixion. It is also the color of fire, so red can be used on Pentecost Sunday along with yellow.

YELLOW or GOLD is generally seen as a color of joy and is used on celebration days like Easter, Epiphany, Christmas, and Pentecost.

GREEN is generally seen as the color of the Holy Ghost and a symbol of life eternal. It is often used after Easter and Epiphany, to mark the time when the early church was growing.

BLACK is seen as a color of mourning. Black is used on Good Friday to mark Jesus' crucifixion. It is also acceptable to remove all color from the sanctuary on Good Friday.

VIOLET is generally used during the seasons of Lent and Advent. Violet is a color of penance, humility, and melancholy. These seasons are generally used as a time of self-examination, prayer, and doing good works.

WHITE represents light, innocence, purity, and joy—and in this last respect, can be used in combination with yellow. White is the accepted color for Christmas and can also be used on Easter.

BLUE is often thought of as Mary's color—and has replaced violet as the prominent color for Advent in some traditions. It is also the color of the sky and can be used in any worship service where green is used. A deeper blue can be used on holidays that require introspection, as in, "Mary took these things and pondered them in her heart" (Luke 2:19).

Holy Week is a great time for liturgical color enthusiasts. Many churches begin with YELLOW on Palm Sunday, switching to GREEN during the week, RED for Maundy Thursday, BLACK on Good Friday, and then WHITE on Easter morning.

Color is important. It can affect our emotions and make us think and react in certain ways. Try to explore these qualities in your worship life with youth. If you have the time and resources, deck out your youth room in various colors according to the church year. Wear a blue T-shirt when leading a worship experience about Mary. These are subtle nuances of worship, yes. But everything we can do to help make the connection is a good thing.

The Sixth Sense in Worship

"I see dead people." No, I'm not talking about the movie with Bruce Willis and Haley Joel Osment. I'm not even talking about a special service for All Hallows' Eve. I'm talking about those truly moving worship experiences where we feel certain there is something else in the room. And there is!

When we begin our worship with a prayer of invocation, we are literally "invoking" the presence of God in the worship circle through the Holy Spirit. Why are we surprised when the Spirit shows up?

It's great to have a unique worship service that opens youth up to new and deeper understandings of God. But even more, what you want is to create opportunities in worship where your youth can feel truly moved by the Spirit. This "sense" of the presence of the holy is not uncommon. It's the goal. God is here, all around us, and worship is a way we connect to God.

Sometimes God connects right back to us, and we feel a "rush" or an "unleashing" of feelings. I once sat in a worship service at the National Youth Workers Convention and experienced what I can only describe as an "emotional toilet flush." I was working in a dysfunctional church at the time, and as I sat there listening to Ken Medema sing and hearing Mike Yaconelli pray and feeling a connection to all the other people in the room and sensing the Holy Spirit moving through the people, I suddenly began to weep. A year's worth of stress and anger and fear suddenly overflowed in me, and I felt this incredible emptiness, which was immediately followed by a sense of "filling" that was warm and gentle and compassionate.

If these God-moments happen during a worship service you've planned… let them happen. Put your arms around those who are feeling these emotions. When you begin using all five senses in worship, your students will hear the words of God more intimately and will be more intensely moved by the service.

The Services

In this section, you will find nine complete worship services for use with your students. Don't be afraid to adapt these services or use them more than once. Part of the worship process is to feel comfortable and familiar with the practice of worship.

You'll find a wide variety of services. Some have a serious feel; others are quite relaxed. They range in length from just a few minutes to more than an hour. You'll find a few intended to mark specific occasions and others that will work at any place, at any time, with any type of music. Some services require a great deal of preparation (such as the Seder Service), while others can be pulled together quickly with things you'd find at a rest stop on I-71 outside Cleveland (The Roadside Service).

Each of the services is intended to function as a starting point. Feel free to incorporate your own ideas and change the music, prayers, and other elements to suit your situation.

A Service for the Start of a New School Year

Style	Meditative, celebratory
Location	Location Indoors, possibly a Sunday school room or some other room where you can safely reach the ceiling with a ladder
Length	30 minutes
Materials	Lots of newspapers, tape, markers, boom box
Scripture	Various readings are incorporated into the litanies.
Music Suggestions	For opening music, choose a song with a "something-is-about-to-happen" feel to it. Possibilities include "Make A Joyful Noise/I Will Not Be Silent" by David Crowder Band from their CD *All I Can Say*, or "I Still Haven't Found What I'm Looking For" from U2's *The Joshua Tree*. You might also try "The Lord's My Shepherd" or "Spirit, Draw Near" from the CD included with this book. Close with music that has a "can't-keep-a-good-man-down" feel. I've led this service using "Change in My Life" by John Pagano (off the *Leap of Faith* soundtrack) and "Lions" off the *This* CD by Lost and Found.
Comments/Ideas	If you have a talented drummer in your group, you might want to ask that person to provide a steady background beat on a wastebasket during the reading portion of this service. Be sure to work with your drummer ahead of time on this.

Introduction

This service symbolizes the fact that we worship a God of new beginnings and second chances. You can use this service as a way to celebrate the new school year—as an affirmation to give hope to those who dread or fear another school year, as well as an encouragement for those who love school and all its possibilities. The service can also be modified for use when a youth leader begins work with a new church and youth group.

Before the service itself begins, you'll want to build a "wall" in the center of the youth room with newspaper or butcher paper from your craft closet. Using strong tape, secure sheets of paper to the ceiling of the room. Tape sheets of paper together until you can tape the bottom sheet to the floor. Continue until you have literally "walled off" half of the room. (It may be easier to measure the room first and build the wall on the floor, and then secure it to the floor and ceiling.) During the service itself, you will need a utility knife to cut a door into the wall.

Order of Worship

Responsive Reading

This opening reading contains a collection of statements likely to be familiar to most of the youth in your group. Each line spoken by the Leader invites a well-known response. If you can avoid printing this reading out for your group, do so.

It is most effective if responses are spoken by the group from memory, rather than read.

Leader: The Lord be with you.

People: And also with you.

Leader: The Lord is my shepherd.

People: I shall not want.

Leader: God is great.

People: God is good.

Leader: Love is patient.

People: Love is kind.

Leader: Now I lay me down to sleep.

People: I pray the Lord my soul to keep.

Leader: Praise God from whom all blessings flow.

People: Praise him all creatures here below.

You can incorporate into this litany lines from other Scriptures, prayers, or worship rituals that your youth would recognize. But use only two lines from any particular source.

Opening Meditation

The Leader should say something like:

One thing this school year is *not* is just another school year. You are not headed back to the same old school to see the same old teachers and eat in the same old cafeteria. This school year is not just "more of the same." This school year is the beginning of something new.

It's like when a family has a second child. That second child is *never* born into the same family as the first child. A first child is born into a family that has no children, but a second child is born to a family that has experience. In the same way, this school year is a new beginning for you. Everything is brand new—if you choose to see it that way.

God spoke to the prophet Isaiah and said, "See, I am doing a new thing!" Jesus did not say, "I came so all things could be…uh…pretty much the same as they always have been." Jesus said, "I came so that all things could be NEW."

As we read and hear the following Scriptures, understand they are all "beginnings." Each of them represents a fresh start, a second chance. We need to hear them continue. And like the first day of school, all a beginning requires is that you keep going.

Scripture Readings

If youth leaders are leading this service for your group, have them stand in a circle around the youth. The readings can be done by just two readers, or can be divided to match as many as are willing to read—the more voices, the better. Readers can be adults or youth and should include both guys and girls. Verses should be read one at a time, but without leaving space between the readings.

{ 22 }

Reader 1: In the beginning God created the heavens and the earth. Now the earth was formless and empty, darkness was over the surface of the deep, and the Spirit of God was hovering over the waters.

Reader 2: So God created man in his own image, in the image of God he created him; male and female he created them.

Reader 1: So the Lord said, "I will wipe mankind, whom I have created, from the face of the earth—men and animals, and creatures that move along the ground, and birds of the air—for I am grieved that I have made them." But Noah found favor in the eyes of the Lord.

Reader 2: Then they said, "Come, let us build ourselves a city, with a tower that reaches to the heavens, so that we may make a name for ourselves and not be scattered over the face of the whole earth."

Reader 1: The Lord had said to Abram, "Leave your country, your people and your father's household and go to the land I will show you. I will make you into a great nation."

Reader 2: Now Israel loved Joseph more than any of his other sons, because he had been born to him in his old age; and he made a richly ornamented robe for him. When his brothers saw that their father loved him more than any of them, they hated him and could not speak a kind word to him.

Reader 1: Then Pharaoh's daughter saw the basket among the reeds and sent her slave girl to get it. She opened it and saw the baby. He was crying, and she felt sorry for him. "This is one of the Hebrew babies," she said.

Reader 2: But Ruth replied, "Don't urge me to leave you or to turn back from you. Where you go I will go, and where you stay I will stay. Your people will be my people and your God my God. Where you die I will die, and there I will be buried. May the Lord deal with me, be it ever so severely, if anything but death separates you and me."

Reader 1: Goliath stood and shouted to the ranks of Israel, "Why do you come out and line up for battle? Am I not a Philistine, and are you not the servants of Saul? Choose a man and have him come down to me."

Reader 2: Then the Lord said to Satan, "Have you considered my servant Job? There is no one on earth like him; he is blameless and upright, a man who fears God and shuns evil."

Reader 1: There is a time for everything, and a season for every activity under heaven:

Reader 2: a time to be born and a time to die,

Reader 1: a time to plant and a time to uproot,

Reader 2: a time to kill and a time to heal,

Reader 1: a time to tear down and a time to build,

Reader 2: a time to weep and a time to laugh,

Reader 1: a time to mourn and a time to dance,

Reader 2: a time to scatter stones and a time to gather them,

Reader 1: a time to embrace and a time to refrain,

Reader 2: a time to search and a time to give up,

Reader 1: a time to keep and a time to throw away,

Reader 2: a time to tear and a time to mend,

Reader 1: a time to be silent and a time to speak,

Reader 2: a time to love and a time to hate,

Reader 1: a time for war and a time for peace.

Reader 2: Then Daniel went to Arioch, whom the king had appointed to execute the wise men of Babylon, and said to him, "Do not execute the wise men of Babylon. Take me to the king, and I will interpret his dream for him."

Reader 1: "See, I will send my messenger, who will prepare the way before me. Then suddenly the Lord you are seeking will come to his temple; the messenger of the covenant, whom you desire, will come," says the Lord Almighty.

Reader 2: This is how the birth of Jesus Christ came about: His mother Mary was pledged to be married to Joseph, but before they came together, she was found to be with child through the Holy Spirit.

Reader 1: John wore clothing made of camel's hair, with a leather belt around his waist, and he ate locusts and wild honey. And this was his message: "After me will come one more powerful than I, the thongs of whose sandals I am not worthy to stoop down and untie. I baptize you with water, but he will baptize you with the Holy Spirit."

Reader 2:

The Word was first,

the Word present to God,

God present to the Word.

The Word was God,

in readiness for God from day one.

Reader 1:

Everything was created through him;

Nothing—not one thing!—

came into being without him.

What came into existence was Life,

and the Life was Light to live by.

Reader 2:

The Life-Light blazed out of the darkness;

the darkness couldn't put it out.

Reader 1: The Word became flesh and blood, and moved into the neighborhood.

Reader 2: Then he told them many things in parables, saying: "A farmer went out to sow his seed. As he was scattering the seed, some fell along the path, and the birds came and ate it up. Some fell on rocky places, where it did not have much soil. It sprang up quickly, because the soil was shallow."

Reader 1: "Therefore, the kingdom of heaven is like a king who wanted to settle accounts with his servants. As he began the settlement, a man who owed him ten thousand talents was brought to him."

Reader 2: "For the kingdom of heaven is like a landowner who went out early in the morning to hire men to work in his vineyard. He agreed to pay them a denarius for the day and sent them into his vineyard."

Reader 1: "The kingdom of heaven is like a king who prepared a wedding banquet for his son. He sent his servants to those who had been invited to the banquet to tell them to come, but they refused to come."

Reader 2: "Again, it will be like a man going on a journey, who called his servants and entrusted his property to them. To one he gave five talents of money, to another two talents, and to another one talent, each according to his ability. Then he went on his journey."

Reader 1: In reply Jesus said: "A man was going down from Jerusalem to Jericho, when he fell into the hands of robbers. They stripped him of his clothes, beat him and went away, leaving him half dead."

Reader 2: Then Jesus told them this parable: "Suppose one of you has a hundred sheep and loses one of them. Does he not leave the ninety-nine in the open country and go after the lost sheep until he finds it?"

Reader 1: Jesus continued: "There was a man who had two sons. The younger one said to his father, 'Father, give me my share of the estate.' So he divided his property between them."

Reader 2: Then he took the cup, gave thanks and offered it to them, saying, "Drink from it, all of you. It is my blood."

Reader 1: Thinking he was the gardener, she said, "Sir, if you have carried him away, tell me where you have put him, and I will get him." Jesus said to her, "Mary." She turned toward him and cried out in Aramaic, "Rabboni!" (which means Teacher).

Reader 2: Mary Magdalene went to the disciples with the news: "I have seen the Lord!" And she told them that he had said these things to her.

Reader 1: And Jesus said, "Behold, I am with you...always."

Reader 2: And Jesus said, "Behold, I am with you...always."

All voices (stagger these voices so they sound like echoes):

I am with you...always.

The Wall

The Leader should say the following:

This is a chance. This is a new beginning. Right now you can choose to look at this new school year with all the potential and hope that God sees in you. You can look at this school year as an opportunity. Look at this wall. It represents all that is keeping you back. Think of all the things that are separating you from what you want to be, from what God wants you to be. I'm going to cut a door in this wall, and then each of you is going to step through, one at a time. As you step through, I want you to say the words: "God makes all things new."

At this point take the utility knife and cut a door into the wall you have created. Do not cut all the way down to the floor. Open the door and invite the students to step through one at a time.

Closing Prayer

Close with this prayer or one of your own.

Creator God, you have given us so much potential. Forgive us when we waste it. Open the doors; show us the light. Let us begin again. Let us see every day as a gift. Let us use all you have given us. Let us hear your voice and see your face. Let us go from this place as new creations. Amen.

Sending Music

A Service of Blessing for a New Youth Room

Style	Dedication
Location	The service begins outside the new youth space, and then moves into the space.
Length	15 minutes
Materials	A brand new Bible, some water in a chalice, some sort of sacred object such as a candle or piece of art, materials for communion
Scripture	Various readings are incorporated into the litanies.
Music Suggestions	If your youth group has a "theme song" or any other particular favorite, use that song. If not, choose something that sounds celebratory and the youth can dance to. Try "No One Like You" by David Crowder Band on their *Illuminate* CD. For fun, you might try "Barometer Soup" on Jimmy Buffett's CD of the same name. Or, if you want something more traditional (but still edgy), check out Lost and Found's *Speedwood Hymns* CD.
Comments/Ideas	Get as much participation as you can on this one. The litany includes parts for one or more readers that can be assigned before you begin.

Introduction

If you're at a church long enough (or if your youth group changes size dramatically), you may have the pleasure of getting a new youth room. It may be a brand new space in an entirely new building—or it may be a storeroom that's been cleaned out and dubbed the "new" youth room. Either way, it's important to let your students know this new space is a gift from God for his good works. Gather the youth together and hold this quick but moving service of dedication.

Order of Worship

The service begins with the group gathered outside the door of the new youth room.

Responsive Reading

Leader: Let the door be opened.

Group: Peace be on this house and all who enter here, in the name of the Father, the Son, and the Holy Spirit.

Reader: Lord Jesus, make this a temple of your presence and a house of prayer. Be near us when we seek you in this place. Draw us to you when we come alone and when we gather with others. May this room be a place where we find comfort and wisdom, where we are supported and strengthened, where we rejoice and give thanks. In this place, Jesus, join us together and make us one with you, so our lives are sustained and blessed for your service.

Leader: *(Placing his/her hand on the door)* **There is one God, one faith, and one Spirit.**

All: *(Placing hands upon the door)* Thanks be to God.

Everyone enters. After everyone is settled, a candle, cross, or other sacred object can be placed in the room.

Leader: Father, may all who gather here come to know and understand your Son Jesus and the great love you have for us. May we hear your voice in the music and the Word. May we feel your presence in the voices and the laughter.

All: Thanks be to God.

A new Bible is placed in the room.

Reader: May all who enter this place hear from this book and learn.

All: Thanks be to God.

A container of water is presented, and water is sprinkled around the room.

Leader: May justice roll down like a mighty river in this place, and love and mercy run through it like an ever-flowing stream.

Scripture

One or more of the following Scriptures can be read:

Exodus 35:30-36:5

Psalm 48

Psalm 84

1 Corinthians 3:10-17

Communion [level 2]

Communion may be served in the new room.

Benediction

Leader: Almighty Father, we thank you for feeding us with the body and blood of your Son and for uniting us in him through the gathering with your Holy Spirit. We ask that you would be with us in this place. May it be a shelter as you are a shelter. May it be a refuge as you are a refuge. May it be a place where you are honored, and where we find the strength and encouragement to live out your Word.

All: Amen.

Closing Music

Play the celebratory music you selected.

The Services

Seder Service and Meal

Style	Experiential, serious through most of the meal, celebrative at the end
Location	Indoors, seated on the floor in a circle (or multiple circles if the group is large)
Length	About an hour
Materials	Large plate, pitcher of water, cups for all, two cups of wine or juice, small bowl of water (for symbolic hand washing), small dish of water mixed with salt, prepared seder foods (see below), celebrative food, candles (one for the center of the room plus others)
Scripture	Exodus 1:12-14; 6:6; 12:17; 13:3; Deuteronomy 16:3; Psalm 119:103-107
Music Suggestions	While the seder itself does not feature music, you can use music as youth gather and for the closing celebration. To set the mood, you might try soundtrack music from either *The Prince of Egypt* or Mel Gibson's *The Passion of the Christ*. You might also use "Table of Christ" or "Love Theme" from the *Spirit, Draw Near* CD included with this book. You can use klezmer music for the celebration at the end of the service. (Try something from The Klezmatics.) For a more contemporary feel, try "Come and Listen" or "Foreverandever Etc..." off the David Crowder Band CD titled *A Collision*.
Comments/Ideas	This modified and simplified version of a traditional Jewish Passover seder celebrates the Jewish heritage of the Christian faith and gives youth a taste of the Passover meal Jesus ate with his disciples in the upper room.

Introduction

The celebration of the Passover through a ceremonial dinner known as a seder is one of the most cherished and widely practiced traditions in the Jewish faith. It is a ritual rich in history and meaning. Jesus and his disciples were celebrating the Passover seder on the night he was betrayed. It was bread and wine from the seder meal that Jesus shared with his disciples in establishing the Christian practice of the Lord's Supper.

This modified seder service is presented with great respect for the Jewish faith, recognizing that our own Christian faith flows out of Judaism. *The service is by no means authentic*—an authentic Jewish seder involves 15 courses and would require more space and explanation than is available here. But the service is intended to celebrate the Jewish roots of our Christian faith and to give your youth a sense of the meal Jesus and his friends experienced on the night before the crucifixion.

The traditional seder is a family celebration. In this adapted seder service, the words and actions of the "Leader" are modeled on the role performed by the father in most Jewish families. The "Reader" speaks words similar to those that would be spoken by the mother.

Food Preparation

The seder is a long service that involves much preparation. Out of respect for Jewish tradition, all preparation for this service must be done before sundown.

You will want to prepare a large seder plate for the meal. If your group is large you may need to prepare one plate for every five or six students, and designate an adult in each group who will serve as a leader. The ingredients should be placed along the perimeter of the plate, leaving the center of the plate open for God.

Each seder plate should include the following:

- matzo (unleavened bread)

- a small dish of water mixed with salt (symbolizing tears)

- maror (bitter herbs) You can use horseradish (symbolizing slavery).

- karpas (vegetable) You can use fresh parsley or pieces of cooked potato.

- charoset (apples, nuts, and cinnamon or brown sugar, all mashed together into a paste) (symbolizes the mortar the slaves used between the bricks)

- zeora (lambbone) If lamb is not easily available, you can use a chicken drumstick with the meat cooked and cut off the bone into small pieces.

- bitzah (cooked egg) Cook the egg any way you like, but then cut it into small pieces. It is a symbol of grief, as well as a symbol of new life.

In addition to the seder plate, you'll need a bowl that will be filled with water for hand washing, a pitcher of water with cups for all to drink, two glasses of juice or wine, and "celebration food" to be passed out as the service concludes. For the celebration food, use some sort of food that symbolizes joy and celebration. Don't use store-bought cookies unless your kids really love Oreos and milk. You can use Ben & Jerry's ice cream or homemade cookies—any kind of sweet food your group enjoys.

Order of Worship

The service begins with the participants seated in a circle on the floor around the Passover plate and an unlit candle. Several other unlit candles should be placed around the room.

Leader: Welcome. Let us make our hearts ready to celebrate. Let us tell the story of the exodus. Let us tell the story of freedom. Let us tell the story of redemption. Imagine what it was like to be a slave in Egypt. Imagine what it was like to walk in darkness. We must be able to imagine these things in order to celebrate the story of the exodus as our own story. It is in this spirit of community that we enter into this celebration of the Passover.

Reader: Our meal contains no leaven. No yeast. In putting away the leaven, we symbolize our willingness to obey God. As we have removed the chametz, the leaven, from our meal, let us think on the things in our hearts that keep us from knowing God.

Leader: We thank and praise you, our Father and Creator of the universe, who commanded that we celebrate the Passover by removing the leaven.

People: Just as the leaven is removed from this meal, may the obstacles we place between ourselves and God be removed.

The center candle is lit.

Leader: May this now be a holy space.

Reader: We are gathered here in the presence of friends and family. Before us are the symbols of our sacred celebration. We are here, old and young, linking the past and present and future of our people. We tell the story that has not yet concluded.

People: "Celebrate the Feast of Unleavened Bread, because it was on this very day that I brought your divisions out of Egypt. Celebrate this day as a lasting ordinance for the generations to come" (Exodus 12:17).

Reader: We assemble in fulfillment of the commandment:

People: "Then Moses said to the people, 'Commemorate this day, the day you came out of Egypt, out of the land of slavery, because the Lord brought you out of it with a mighty hand. Eat nothing containing yeast'" (Exodus 13:3).

Reader: God, Creator of the universe, you saved us from death so we may celebrate life. As we light these candles, we pray for your light in this place, so we may see the significance of this celebration.

People: God of second chances, let these lights inspire strength—to love and not to hate, to bless and not to curse, and to serve and to worship you.

Pass out matches or tapers and light the other candles around the room.

Leader: Our story is told again and again with different words. God promises his people freedom. With the four mouthfuls of water, we celebrate God's promises to us.

The Leader takes the pitcher of water and pours a small amount of water into his cup four times. Others do the same. This is a symbolic action and does not require a lot of water to be poured each time. After water has been poured into every cup, the Leader holds his glass up and says:

Leader: Tonight we celebrate the four "I will" promises God made to his people.

All people hold up their glasses and say:

All: "I am the Lord. I will bring you out of the yoke of the Egyptians. I will deliver you from slavery. I will redeem you with an outstretched arm. I will take you as my people" (Exodus 6:6).

Leader: We take the cup and proclaim this to be a holy day. God keeps his promises. God is faithful to those who trust in him. In every age there are oppressors who would work to keep us under their feet. From the hands of those who would hold us down, God will deliver us. Thank you, God, for freedom.

All may drink.

{ 33 }

Leader: We now prepare for the meal by washing our hands, symbolizing the holiness of this gathering and our desire that we would live out our calling as God's children with our hearts and our hands.

The Leader takes the large bowl and pours water into it from the pitcher. One at a time, everyone dips their hands into the water to clean them symbolically. Again, a large amount of water is not necessary.

When this is finished, the Leader takes the piece of parsley or potato and holds it up for all to see.

Leader: This is karpas. It represents all the good things in life that God, the Creator, has given us. Because God loves us, we are filled with love and joy. And yet this good life that God intended is often mixed with tears.

The Leader lifts up the bowl of salt water so all can see.

Leader: Tonight, we are celebrating the freedom and wonderful deliverance that God brought to us as slaves in Egypt. We must not forget that our lives as slaves were full of hardship and suffering and tears. We must not forget that the struggle for freedom begins with tears.

People: Blessed are you, O God.

Everyone dips the vegetable into the salt water and eats it.

Leader: The breaking of the matzo in two is a symbol that we are in community with others who share in this celebration—all people... everywhere...around the world.

The Leader breaks the matzo in half. Others do the same.

Leader: We tell the story that joins us together. We are one with our families, with our friends, and with the beggar on the street. God's grace breaks the bonds that hold us to those who would oppress us.

People: This is the bread of affliction. Our ancestors ate it in the land of Egypt. Let all who are hungry eat. Let all who are needy celebrate. Now we are slaves. Let us pray that we may truly be free.

The Story of the Passover

People: We were once slaves. Then God stretched out his arm and brought us from the land of Egypt.

Leader: God has rescued us. If it were not for God, we and our children and our children's children would still be slaves, our freedom and dignity stolen from us.

People: Once we worshiped idols and false gods. God, the one God, the Creator God, forgives us and calls us to be his children.

Leader: Tonight is different from all other nights. Tonight we gather to remember who we are and what God has done for us, and to pass on the story of God's grace.

People: God is in all places and in all things. God is everywhere. Praise be to God who gave us freedom.

Reader: God promised Abraham and Sarah they would bring forth generation after generation of people. God made this same promise to Isaac and to Jacob. Jacob's children came to the land of Egypt where Jacob's son Joseph became the advisor to Pharaoh. But years went by, and a new government came into power. Its leaders did not remember Joseph. They did not remember Joseph's God. These leaders forced the Israelites to become slaves and to work making bricks. As the Israelites' numbers increased, Pharaoh feared they might overtake his kingdom. So he ordered that all newborn Israelite boys be drowned. Our ancestors knew only tears and sorrow.

Leader: They cried out to God and begged him to remember the promises he made to Abraham. God heard them, and through the actions of a wise mother and her sister, he saved the life of one

baby boy. That was Moses. When Moses became an adult, God sent him back to Egypt to deliver his people from slavery.

Reader: When Moses asked Pharaoh to free his people, Pharaoh refused. So God sent 10 plagues on the land of Egypt.

The Leader takes the first cup of juice and holds it.

Leader: As we recount the 10 plagues God sent to Egypt, we place a drop of wine on the plate.

As each item on the list is read, the Leader dips a finger into the cup and places a drop of juice on the plate.

Leader: Blood. Frogs. Lice. Swarms. Cattle Disease. Boils. Hail. Locusts. Darkness. Death of the Firstborn.

Reader: Pharaoh still refused to let the people go. So God sent the plague of death. God instructed the people to sacrifice a lamb and to paint the blood of the lamb on the doorframes of all the Israelites. Those who had the blood of the lamb on their doors were "passed over" when the plague of death came through the kingdom.

The Leader removes the zeora (drumstick) from the seder plate and holds it up for everyone to see.

Leader: This is the symbol of the lamb, sacrificed so our children would live.

{ 35 }

All taste a bite of the meat. Next, the Leader takes the roasted egg from the seder plate and holds it up for all to see.

Leader: The egg is a symbol of sadness and grief. It reminds us the temple of our ancestors is no longer standing. The egg has no beginning and no end. So it is also a symbol of life and hope. It reminds us the love of God is unending and cannot be confined to a temple.

Everyone tastes some of the egg.

Reader: Even as the children of Israel were leaving, Pharaoh changed his mind and sent his armies after Moses and his people. God told Moses to lift his staff over the sea; he did so, and the waters of the sea parted, allowing the children of Israel to pass safely through. When Pharaoh's armies tried to follow, God allowed the waters to close over them. When the people saw what had happened and knew they were free, they rejoiced, praising God and saying...

People: Praise God. Praise God, Creator of the universe. God hears his children cry and brings them out of slavery.

Leader: Tonight we eat unleavened bread because our ancestors in Egypt had to leave in a hurry and could not even wait for the bread to rise. It baked while it was still flat.

People: "Do not eat it with bread made with yeast, but for seven days eat unleavened bread, the bread of affliction, because you left Egypt in haste—so that all the days of your life you may remember the time of your departure from Egypt" (Deuteronomy 16:3).

The Leader breaks the matzo into smaller pieces. Each person at the table takes a piece of the matzo and dips it into the maror (horseradish).

Leader: Tonight we eat bitter herbs to remind us of our lives as slaves. No matter how sweet life gets, we must never forget the bitterness of slavery.

People: "But the more they were oppressed, the more they multiplied and spread; so the Egyptians came to dread the Israelites and worked them ruthlessly. They made their lives bitter with hard labor in brick and mortar and with all kinds of work in the fields; in all their hard labor the Egyptians used them ruthlessly" (Exodus 1:12-14).

Everyone tastes the matzo and maror. When all have eaten, the Leader takes another piece of matzo and dips it in the charoset (the apple mixture). Everyone does the same.

Leader: We dipped in the maror to remind us of life's bitterness, and now we dip in the charoset to remind us life is also sweet and God can bring sweetness into the bitterest of circumstances.

People:

How sweet are your words to my taste,

sweeter than honey to my mouth!

I gain understanding from your precepts;

therefore I hate every wrong path.

Your word is a lamp to my feet

and a light for my path.

I have taken an oath and confirmed it,

that I will follow your righteous laws.

I have suffered much;

preserve my life, O Lord, according to your word.

(Psalm 119:103-107)

Everyone tastes the charoset.

Leader: Tonight is a celebration. We eat with special rituals because each generation must feel connected to the slaves who came out of Egypt. We tell the story because God has forgiven us and kept his promises. We can sing a new song.

People: We were slaves, but now we are free.

The Leader takes the second glass and raises it for everyone to see.

Leader: With the second cup we celebrate that God has taken us out of slavery and brought us into freedom. We thank God for his grace, his freedom, and his choice to bring us out of sorrow and into joy.

People: We praise you, God, who has freed your people.

Leader: We praise you God, Creator of all things.

Everyone drinks from the second cup.

Leader: Our seder is now complete, just as our redemption is complete. We rejoice with thanksgiving, yet we are humbled by God's love! We raise our glasses again in thanksgiving for God's grace and love.

People: Blessed are you, God, Creator of the universe, who has adopted us and allowed us to call you Father.

All drink from the second cup again.

Leader: For centuries people have concluded the seder meal with the expression: "Next Year In Jerusalem." We will conclude our seder this way. We hope and have faith in God as we await the future: Next Year in the New Jerusalem.

People: Next Year in the New Jerusalem!

The service concludes with celebrative music and food.

Hard Communion Service

Style Informal, experiential

Location Outdoors. Hike in the woods or climb out on your church roof. Get out of the building. Pick a place that takes some effort to get to.

Length If you're going to make your own bread for this service (see the recipes below), then the whole process will take a couple of hours. The service itself will take 20 or 30 minutes.

Materials Homemade bread and wine (juice), Bibles, "hard communion" cup (Use a wooden cup if you have it; otherwise, use a beat-up coffee mug with a broken handle.)

Scripture Matthew 26:26-29; Mark 14:22-25; Luke 22:19-20; John 14:23; 1 Corinthians 10:16-17; 11:24-26; Ephesians 4:1-6

Music Suggestions Try using "God Above" from the *Spirit, Draw Near* disc as an opener. You might also use "Come Thou Fount" (acoustic version) or another track from David Crowder Band's *All I Can Say* CD. Other options would include just about anything from *Speedwood Hymns* by Lost and Found or the *Enter the Worship Circle* CDs. Jeff Johnson's *Benediction* has some nice Celtic-sounding look-at-the-stars tunes.

Comments/Ideas This service is most effective if the youth have made the elements for the service—or at least the bread, which can be done immediately prior to the service itself. Be sure your kids know the making of the elements is part of the worship. Encourage all of them to get their hands dirty. For Scriptures from Matthew, Mark, and Luke, use a King James Version Bible—preferably an old one with marred and yellowed pages. It adds to the mood of the service. When your students read the Scriptures, have them pay attention to the subtle differences in the way the different Gospel writers chose to write about the Last Supper.

Introduction

The communion service is probably a staple in your church. Maybe your congregation takes communion once a month; maybe you celebrate the Eucharist every Sunday. Either way, your students are probably familiar with the process by now.

Jesus didn't take his disciples into the upper room for the purpose of holding a communion service.

They were there to celebrate the Passover with a seder meal (see the service on page **, which can be used in combination with this one). But he took the wine and bread from that traditional Jewish meal and invested them with new meaning and significance. Jesus said, "Do this in remembrance of me" (Luke 22:19). And we have.

This small ritual that began with a man who never made it more than a few miles out of his hometown is now observed across the planet. Christians all over the world practice communion. In some places, the communion service includes a full mass choir and much ritual and pageantry. In other places, you could, quite literally, be arrested and killed for holding communion.

In most U.S. churches, communion services have gotten too pretty. We get out the white silk cloths and the shiny gold or silver trays. You might use communion wafers or small bits of pita bread or Wonder Bread cut into tiny squares. We use "the good plates" and the altar cloths to show reverence for the service. This service changes that.

"Hard Communion" means we are going to make the traditional communion service more experiential. We are going to use all five senses. We are going to get out of the church. And we won't be using Wonder Bread cubes, Welch's juice, and white linen napkins.

Spend time in the afternoon making the bread and the juice. Get all your students involved. You can make the elements as a group activity at one time, and then hold the service at a later date. Or you can do it all in one shot and take warm bread and fresh juice with you when you get out of the building.

Hard Communion Recipes

Get your students involved in the process of making the bread and juice for communion. Ideally, the juice should be made at least three months in advance and stored. (It's great to make the juice in the summer and use it that winter for the communion service.) If time permits, the bread can be made on the same day as the service itself.

Remember that this is also a wonderful opportunity to talk about what the Eucharist really means. Sometimes it's easier to talk when your hands are busy. You can say things while doing the dishes that you can't say at the dinner table. Ask your students about what they believe when they are up to their wrists in flour, and you'll get a better response.

Communion Bread

Ingredients

1 tsp. dry yeast (check date on packet)

2½ cups warm water (about 105 degrees)

1 cup wheat flour

1 cup rye flour

4 cups all-purpose white flour

1 tbsp. salt

2 tbsp. dark olive oil

Directions

In a large bowl, gently mix water and yeast.

One cup at a time, add rye, wheat, and ONE cup of white flour.

Stir with hands about 100 times in the same direction.

Let rest for about an hour.

Sprinkle salt over this "sponge" and stir in olive oil.

Mix in remaining white flour one cup at a time. Stir with hands or wooden spoon.

When dough is too stiff to mix, drop onto a floured breadboard and knead for 10 minutes until smooth.

Let dough rise until doubled in size (takes about 1½ to 2 hours).

Divide dough into chunks. This dough will make about 16 pita-sized loaves of bread. Roll gently into balls and flatten with rolling pin.

Bake at 450 degrees for 8 to 10 minutes or until golden.

Note: The loaves may "puff up," but that's normal. Do not overbake. After bread cools, keep it in plastic bags until you are ready to lead the service.

Communion Juice

You will need a canner and canning jars to make this juice. Don't try to do it without a canner. The bottom of a regular pot would get too hot and break your jars. (There may be a canner hanging out in your church kitchen somewhere, or perhaps you can borrow one from a church member who might also help you make this juice.)

Ingredients

Grapes or other fruit (Red grapes are probably your best bet. It's also possible to use white or purple grapes, but it's not a good idea not to mix different varieties. You can also use raspberries or blackberries.)

Sugar

Directions

Bring water to a boil in the canner. Boil a second pot of water for use in the juice.

Place the jars in boiling water for several minutes.

Remove the jars (use tongs).

Dump ½ cup of crushed fruit and ½ cup of sugar into each jar.

Using boiling water from the second pot, fill each jar to within ½ inch.

Put on scalded lids and tighten with rings.

Place jars in canner. Cover with water and boil for 20 minutes.

Carefully remove jars and set on counter. Re-tighten lids.

Allow the juice to sit for at least three months. This is a great summer activity that will come back into play when you take your winter retreat.

Order of Worship

Choose an outdoor location for your service, a place that takes some time and effort to get to. Once you arrive, take a moment and allow the group to sit and rest in silence. Play one of the music suggestions or one of your own choosing.

Make sure your group knows this is not "social time." It is worship.

Opening Prayer

God of the sky and stars and earth and rock, we come to you now in this time and in this place to remember your Son. Make your presence known to us here, now in a very real and concrete way. Give us a break from the noise and chaos and make us remember we are taking your Son into ourselves, that by participating in this service now, we are asking Jesus to become a part of who we are—now and every day. Amen.

Responsive Reading

After each line read by the Leader, let the people respond, "And I have turned away from you, Lord."

Leader: I have made big mistakes.

Group: And I have turned away from you, Lord.

Leader: I knew what I was doing.

Group: And I have turned away from you, Lord.

Leader: I am not God, though sometimes I act like I think I am.

Group: And I have turned away from you, Lord.

Leader: I have seen horrible things on the news.

Group: And I have turned away from you, Lord.

Leader: I have seen broken people on the street.

Group: And I have turned away from you, Lord.

Leader: I have seen broken people in my house.

Group: And I have turned away from you, Lord.

Leader: There are answers in front of me.

Group: And I have turned away from you, Lord.

Leader: There are solutions in my possession.

Group: And I have turned away from you, Lord.

Leader: I have eyes, ears, a voice, and two hands.

Group: And I have turned away from you, Lord.

{ 42 }   **Leader: I knew full well.**

Group: And I have turned away from you, Lord.

Leader: I thought it was too hard.

Group: And I have turned away from you, Lord.

Leader: I am so far off the path I can't find my way back.

Group: And I have turned away from you, Lord.

Leader: It would be easier if I just stayed lost.

Group: And I have turned away from you, Lord.

All: Amen.

Scriptures

Read the Scriptures from Matthew, Mark, and Luke.

Communion

The youth leader should tell the story of the Last Supper in his or her own words. Point out to the group that this ritual was like a gift Jesus offered to the disciples. Jesus gave them a practice to remember him by. Explain that this ritual occurred after a celebration meal and that Jesus seemed to have used whatever was left on the table. Don't be afraid to rip off a big wad of bread for yourself and to encourage youth to do the same. Urge them to dip the bread deep into the cup and then eat. Encourage them to fully experience the tastes and smells of the Eucharist.

Scriptures

Read the Scriptures from John, 1 Corinthians, and Ephesians.

Responsive Reading

After each line read by the Leader, the group should respond, "I am a servant of God."

Leader's Note: If the weather is not cold and damp, adjust the opening lines to your surroundings at the moment.

Leader: It's cold.

Group: I am a servant of God.

Leader: It's damp.

Group: I am a servant of God.

Leader: I'm ready for the sun again.

Group: I am a servant of God.

Leader: I will get up in the morning.

Group: I am a servant of God.

Leader: I will do what I always do.

Group: I am a servant of God.

Leader: I will do what I have to do.

Group: I am a servant of God.

Leader: Because that is what I do.

Group: I am a servant of God.

Leader: No discussion. No arguing. No bargaining.

Group: I am a servant of God.

Leader: God has called me, and I will go where I am told.

Group: I am a servant of God.

Leader: People can spend their time building obstacles in my path.

Group: I am a servant of God.

Leader: People can spend their time telling me I am wasting mine.

Group: I am a servant of God.

Leader: They don't know what I know.

Group: I am a servant of God.

Leader: They don't know what I am.

Group: I am a servant of God.

Leader: I am healed. I am free. I am forgiven.

Group: I am a servant of God.

All: Amen.

Closing Music

To introduce the song, the Leader might say:

It was a tradition in the time of Jesus to close the Passover meal with a song. Although the Bible does not say so, it's likely Jesus and his disciples followed that tradition and sang at the end of the meal.

For this song, choose a familiar hymn or song that has particular meaning to your group. If you have a guitarist in your group, ask that person to lead. Otherwise, sing a cappella. (Jesus probably did.)

Closing Prayer

God, we stand before you now with the taste of bread and wine on our lips. We feel the presence of your Son in our bodies and in our hearts and in our souls. He is a part of us now, and we are a part of him, and so, we are also a part of you. Fill us with your Spirit, God. Make us into the body of Christ. Amen.

A Service for Good Friday

Style	Meditative
Location	Sanctuary
Length	45 minutes to 1 hour
Materials	Eight-foot cross (see introduction), large hammer, large crescent wrench, boom box, seven candles (with holders)
Scripture	The seven words of Jesus from the cross will be read or sung as part of the service.
Music Suggestions	There are two particularly significant ways in which music might be used in this service:

First, if you have a junior high girl who sings well, it can be tremendously effective to have her stand at the back of the sanctuary at the very beginning of the service and sing "Jesus Loves Me" a cappella as the rest of the group brings the cross into the sanctuary.

Second, this service is most powerful if the seven words of Christ from the cross are sung rather than read. Composer Antonín Dvořák is among the many who have placed the seven words to music. If you have a trained singer within your congregation who could sing these melodies a cappella, it can be very powerful. The words can also be sung in a simple chanting style.

For "mood music" as your congregation is entering, you might have the Jeff Johnson CD *Vespers* playing in the background. You might also try "When I Survey the Wondrous Cross" from the *Spirit, Draw Near* CD with this book, or "Your Memory" (the acoustic version) from Lost and Found's *Something Different*. For closing music, try Ryan Long's "Family" from *Waiting by the Window* or Ben Harper's "Blessed To Be a Witness" from *Diamonds on the Inside*.

Comments/Ideas	Have one of your youth sit out of sight near a microphone. Have that youth strike a large crescent wrench with the side of a metal hammer to simulate the sound of the hammering of nails into the cross.

Introduction

This Good Friday service takes some practice and coordination, but the final effect is quite powerful. If possible, you'll want to have the youth *build* the cross at the front of your sanctuary. If you have a carpenter in your church, see if that person can create a "kit" for building the cross for you so it can be put together and taken apart easily for rehearsals.

There are many opportunities for youth to be involved throughout the service. In addition to the building of the cross, six monologues can be read by various youth. You'll also want six or eight youth to serve as the "crowd voices." Scatter these youth around the sanctuary. Make sure they have a list of the crowd statements. Have them shout out these lines, each person reading a different statement. Then, after the last line has been read, each of them should read all the lines but NOT simultaneously. Scatter the statements by having each person read the list in a different order. The effect in a dark sanctuary is chilling.

Order of Worship

Procession of the Cross

The service begins with one girl singing "Jesus Loves Me" from the back of the sanctuary. (See "Music Suggestions.") Have the other youth process in with the cross (or the pieces of the cross) as she is singing. Those who do not carry the cross can carry seven lit candles. (Be sure you only use seven candles.)

Make sure your singer knows to continue singing "Jesus Loves Me" over and over until the cross is fully erected. Once the group begins to build or set up the cross at the front of the sanctuary, begin the sound effects of the hammer—not too fast and not to a regular beat. When the cross is standing, have the hammering stop and allow your singer to finish the final chorus.

After the cross is built, the six monologue readers kneel around the cross while the rest of the group takes seats in the congregation.

Opening Responsive Reading

If this litany is not printed out for participants, the Leader can instruct the group to respond to each line with the words, "I am far from God."

Leader: It is dark out here.

Group: I am far from God.

Leader: Am I alone?

Group: I am far from God.

Leader: *(softer)* **Am I alone?**

Group: I am far from God.

Leader: The darkness is beneath my skin.

Group: I am far from God.

Leader: The darkness is in my breath.

Group: I am far from God.

Leader: The darkness is in my soul.

Group: I am far from God.

Leader: I don't want to feel like this, God.

Group: I am far from God.

Leader: If I am alone…it is not you who moved.

Group: I am far from God.

Leader: I left you, not the other way around.

Group: I am far from God.

Leader: If you are always close, why don't I feel you here?

Group: I am far from God.

Leader: I'm ready to come home now.

Group: I am far from God.

Leader: Amen.

Crowd Voices

He doesn't look so important now, does he?

He's a criminal. They hung him with the criminals.

Why did they have to beat him?

What did he do to deserve this?

Let's see some miracles now!

Save yourself.

He's no king.

Monologue 1

When I was 11, I was pretty much like every other boy. We rode our bikes everywhere. We collected rocks. We sat and watched the construction guys work the bulldozers for hours. And I used words like "fag" and "fairy" and made fun of kids we said were "gay." Then when I was 13, I started to realize we were talking about me. I didn't say anything to anybody. When I was 15, I was going to tell my parents, but then one Sunday, our minister preached a sermon about homosexuals. A gay bar was opening the next town over, and our minister preached against it. He used words like "abomination."

I didn't say anything to Mom and Dad after that. How do you tell your parents you are going to hell?

The Voice of Jesus

(sung or read)

Father, forgive them, for they know not what they do.

Crowd Voices

God would never let his Son hang like this. This guy's a fake.

You're not God. You're a joke.

Why have the people turned against him?

You said you'd tear down the temple and rebuild it. It's still there!

You are nothing.

What are we going to do now?

If he is the Son of God, why doesn't he save himself?

Extinguishing Candle 1

The reader of Monologue 1 blows out the first candle.

Monologue 2

I never thought I would ever love someone again. I certainly never thought I would ever get married again. See, I married a jerk the first time around—one of those guys who expresses his opinion with his fists. We had a baby and then another. When the kids were in elementary school, Ron started using them as punching bags, so I grabbed the kids one day and left him. They eventually had to send him away to get him to leave us alone. We were alone for a lot of years, and I thought, "This is it. This is all there's going to be." Then I met Mark. Of course, he had his own baggage, as well as two beautiful little girls. He'd gotten married right out of high school and then divorced. Then he'd married again right away, which was too soon. His girls are with him about six months out of the year. Our kids get along. Mostly anyway. I know that the days when I get out of bed and I'm going to see Mark...those are the good days. We even took this sort of pseudo-family vacation. The six of us took a trip together like some sort of dysfunctional Brady Bunch. We went to Niagara Falls. It was nice. The kids got in just one fight, and that was on the way home, because we were all tired and cranky. Mark is starting to talk in commitment terms, talking about how *we* are gonna get the kids through college, and where *we* will go for vacation when the kids are married and have moved away. I think he's going to ask me to marry him.

Voice of Jesus

(sung or read)

Brother, behold your mother. Woman, behold your son.

Crowd Voices

He performed all those miracles. Why doesn't he do one now?

Where are your tricks now, Jesus?

Why doesn't he say anything?

Is he already dead?

He's a fake. A fraud.

Who is that woman?

What are we going to do now?

Let him save himself!

Extinguishing Candle 2

The reader of Monologue 2 blows out the second candle.

Monologue 3

Your Honor, I know this is my third time. I am asking for mercy. I have cleaned up my act. I wasn't in any shape to try to go back to my life the last time I stood here. I'm not the same person, Your Honor. I'm in a program. I haven't had a drink in 75 days. I haven't even been near a bar. The preacher at the church over on Emerson Road gave me a job. I like the preacher. We talk a lot. I wasn't going to buy drugs with the money we took from the old lady. My friend Larry said she had plenty of cash. She was well off. But I need to pay my rent. I give most of my paycheck to my ex so she can raise the baby. She says if I don't pay the child support, I don't get to see our daughter. I'm sorry the woman got hurt—it was Larry who hit her, not me. She even said so. Your Honor, I can't go to prison. I was so close to putting my life back together. I can do it this time. I'm getting help. I still have a job. I am asking the court for another chance. Please.

Voice of Jesus

(sung or read)

Today, you will be with me in paradise.

Crowd Voices

You're a joke, Jesus.

He's losing his mind.

He was God's Son. He was really God's Son.

Look, he bleeds like any other man.

The others are dead. Why is he hanging on?

Make them stop.

That's his mother. How can she watch this?

Show us your miracles now!

Extinguishing Candle 3

The reader of Monologue 3 blows out the third candle.

Monologue 4

Okay, God, you're with me on this one, right? Because I'm gonna need you. Wait...do I have the ring? Okay, I've got the ring. What am I going to say? You know, any help you could give me here would be appreciated, God. A little divine inspiration? Something? Well, just don't leave me, okay? Make her say yes. Well, don't *make* her say yes. Let her say yes on her own. But if you could stick around, I'd appreciate it. Thank you for her, by the way. Thank you for her. She's good for me. This is one of those there's-someone-for-everyone things, right? We're going to grow old together. She's for me, and I'm for her, right? You wouldn't put us together if it wasn't going to last, right? I don't think I've ever been this nervous. Don't leave me on this one. I don't know what I'll do if she doesn't say yes, God. I really don't.

Voice of Jesus

(sung or read)

I thirst.

Crowd Voices

How can he still be alive?

He's dead; he's got to be dead by now.

The soldiers spit on him.

He's no king.

Jesus! Where is this kingdom you promised?

So much blood. So much blood.

What if he was the Son of God?

Extinguishing Candle 4

The reader of Monologue 4 blows out the fourth candle.

Monologue 5

I don't understand how a child can be fine one moment and then burning up with fever the next. Not in this day and age. It's not fair. He had a lot more living to do. It's not fair. Daniel and I, we were thinking we'd never be able to have kids on our own, but still we prayed every day. I prayed three or four times every day for a baby. Some days, it was like my every breath was a prayer. And then it happened. I got pregnant, and Mike was born in the summer. Everybody said it was a miracle. Why would God take a miracle back? That doesn't make sense. You don't take back a miracle. I was just getting to know him. I was just starting to see a personality. Last week when we gave him strained beets, he made a face that looked just like my dad. He was the joy of my life. And now he's gone. Sometimes I wish you had taken me instead. It's not fair. God, *YOU DON'T TAKE BACK A MIRACLE.*

Voice of Jesus

(sung or spoken)

My God, my God, why have you forsaken me?

Crowd Voices

He's dying.

It's almost done.

He's calling on Elijah.

Oh my God, look at the sky.

God is angry with us.

He was the Son of God.

What have we done?

So much blood. So much blood.

Extinguishing Candle 5

The reader of Monologue 5 blows out the fifth candle.

Monologue 6

He just showed up one day. It was a day like any other, and I was buy-ing olives. Everyone said to come hear the new rabbi. So I went along and listened. He spoke with such authority. It was like he knew...he just knew what he was saying was true. Some of the Pharisees started quizzing him, but he answered every question. They were stumped. He blessed the crowd, and as the people started to leave, he looked right at me. I remember those eyes.

I went toward him, and he said, "Do you want to come with us?"

"Where?" I said.

He said, "Does it matter?"

I had to admit, it didn't. I had nothing to go home to, so I went with them. I saw miracles. I saw people with broken legs get up and dance. I saw people who couldn't speak start to sing.

He said he was the One...the Son of God. And there was no question in any of our minds. It was true. He was the One. *(long pause)*

They killed him. He was the Son of God, and they killed him. First they arrested him, then they beat him, then they put him through that joke of a trial, and today they killed him. And do you know what he said? He said, "Forgive them." He wanted God to forgive the people who put him there. Or maybe he wanted God to forgive us because we just stood there and watched.

We had hopes. We thought this was going to be it. But it's over now. It's just over.

Voice of Jesus

(read or sung)

It is finished.

Extinguishing Candle 6

The reader of Monologue 6 blows out the sixth candle.

Closing Responsive Reading

If this litany is not printed out for participants, the Leader can instruct the group to respond to each line with the words, "Send me, God."

Leader: Moses said it.

Group: Send me, God.

Leader: David screamed it.

Group: Send me, God.

Leader: The prophets, the preachers, the missionaries lived it.

Group: Send me, God.

Leader: I am ready to go.

Group: Send me, God.

Leader: Where do you need me to go?

Group: Send me, God.

Leader: I am listening.

Group: Send me, God.

Leader: Your servant is listening.

Group: Send me, God.

Leader: I want this with everything that I am.

Group: Send me, God.

Leader: Heart. Mind. Soul. I am ready.

Group: Send me, God.

Leader: It doesn't matter where.

Group: Send me, God.

Leader: It doesn't matter what I am called to do.

Group: Send me, God.

Leader: I have been sent by God.

Group: Send me, God.

Leader: God knows exactly what he is doing.

Group: Send me, God.

Leader: I am ready to leave.

Group: Send me, God.

Leader: Amen.

Voice of Jesus

(sung or read)

Father, into your hands I commit my spirit.

The Last Candle

Instead of blowing out the last candle, have your Leader act as if he/she is going to blow it out but then decides not to. Have the Leader take one of the unlit candles, light that candle from the single burning candle, and then carry the light from the sanctuary.

Closing Music

During the closing music, have the group enter from the back SLOWLY and then remove the cross, carrying it on their shoulders like a coffin.

Elijah's Cave: Yeah, It's Kinda Like That

Style	Experiential, fun
Location	To give a feel for Elijah's cave experience, try leading this service in a dimly lit space that is just a little too tight for your group to fit comfortably. See the introduction for directions on preparing the space.
Length	20 minutes
Materials	Pop Rocks (one packet for each student), Atomic FireBalls (one for each student), cooler full of ice, ice-cold cans of Sierra Mist, several large fans
Scripture	1 Kings 19:5-13; Psalms 55 and 116
Music Suggestions	On the CD with this book, "Space and Time" makes great mood music as an opener. You might also try "Distant Land" from Lost and Found's *Something* or "Here Is Our King" from *A Collision* by David Crowder Band. "Biscuits" from the *Many Rooms* CD by Agape is a nice hip-hop-style opener. For closing music, I love "Elijah" from Lost and Found's *Something Different* CD. (Two versions of this song are on the CD. I prefer the acoustic one.)
Comments/Ideas	The spark for this service came from a brainstorming session at a gathering of Episcopal Youth Workers of the Diocese of West Texas. Have one of your youth sit out of sight near a microphone. Have that youth strike a large crescent wrench with the side of a metal hammer to simulate the sound of the hammering of nails into the cross.

{ 55 }

The Services

Introduction

This is a fun little service that can be done at a lock-in or on a retreat. Try to create an enclosed cave-like feel by using a small space where your students will feel packed in. Hide the candy and the soda pop from the students' view. Place several large fans around the outside of the room and run the power cords to a central contact strip. Keep this contact strip hidden from the students. Keep the room dimly lit so the fans are hard to see.

Note: This service includes eating Pop Rocks candy and drinking Sierra Mist soda. Undoubtedly, this combination will cause someone to mention the rumor that "Mikey," the child actor who appeared in the famous Life cereal commercial, was said to have died a horrible death as a teenager because he consumed Pop Rocks and Pepsi at the same time. This is a well-known "urban myth" that is completely false. The kid who played Mikey was named John Gilchrist, and he survived into adulthood with- *out his stomach ever exploding. He is now an advertising executive.*

Order of Worship

Invocation

Leader: Let's open with a prayer. Ever-present God, sometimes we know exactly what you want us to do, but still we go running off in the other direction. We know what we are called to do, but we hide because it's too hard, too long, or just too inconvenient to follow your instructions. It's not always easy being your servant, God—but then, you never promised us it would be easy. You never promised you'd solve all our problems—only that you would be beside us as we face them. Thank you for being with us. We are your servants, God. Amen.

Music

Play one of the music suggestions or come up with one of your own.

Scripture

Read Psalm 55 and/or 116.

Elijah's Story

The Leader should introduce the story by saying something like:

Tonight we're going to talk about listening for God—and not just listening, but doing what we are told. So we're going to look at the story of Elijah.

At his point you can begin passing out the Pop Rocks and Atomic FireBalls, but make sure everyone knows not to eat them until you say so. Do not get out the cold Sierra Mist until the second you are ready to use it.

I'm going read the story of Elijah in the cave. When I tell you to do so, I want you to put the items I tell you in your mouth. To set this story up, keep in mind that Elijah was just in a WWE-type battle royale with the priests who worshiped a god named Baal. This contest happened to show the queen whose God was real.

At this point, read or tell the story of the confrontation between Elijah and the prophets of Baal found in 1 Kings 18:1-19:4. (If you read it, use The Message *or any other translation you are comfortable with.) After reading or telling the story through 19:4, stop and say something like:*

At this point Elijah has done everything God has asked of him. But now there's an army out to kill him. As we read the next part of the story, I'm going to ask you to do several things, so pay attention:

1 Kings 19:5-13

(from *The Message*)

Exhausted, he [Elijah] fell asleep under the lone broom bush. Suddenly an angel shook him awake and said, "Get up and eat!" He looked around, and to his surprise, right by his head were a loaf of bread baked on some coals and a jug of water. He ate the meal and went back to sleep.

The angel of God came back, shook him awake again, and said, "Get up and eat some more—you've got a long journey ahead of you."

He got up, ate and drank his fill, and set out. Nourished by that meal, he walked forty days and nights, all the way to the mountain of God, to Horeb. When he got there, he crawled into a cave and went to sleep.

Then the word of God came to him: "So Elijah, what are you doing here?"

"I've been working my heart out for the God-of-the-Angel-Armies," said Elijah. "The people of Israel have abandoned your covenant, destroyed the places of worship, and murdered your prophets. I'm the only one left, and now they're trying to kill me."

Then he was told, "Go, stand on the mountain at attention before God. God will pass by."

A hurricane wind ripped through the mountains and shattered the rocks before God, but God wasn't to be found in the wind;

(At this point flip the switch on the box fans and let them blow.)

after the wind an earthquake,

(Tell your kids to empty the entire packet of Pop Rocks into their mouths. Leave the fans on.)

but God wasn't in the earthquake; and after the earthquake fire,

(Tell your students to put the Atomic FireBall in their mouth with the Pop Rocks. Have a wastebasket on hand if kids want to spit out the FireBall. Allow the noise and laughter to go on for a few minutes, and eventually turn off the fans and try to get your kids calmed down. Allow spitting if necessary.)

but God wasn't in the fire; and after the fire a gentle and quiet whisper.

(Break out the bottles or cans of Sierra Mist. Allow kids to drink and spit out the FireBall if they wish. Repeat the following line several times.)

But God wasn't in the fire, and after the fire a gentle whisper.

When Elijah heard the quiet voice, he muffled his face with his great cloak, went to the mouth of the cave, and stood there. A quiet voice asked, "So Elijah, now tell me, what are you doing here?"

(Give your group a moment to calm down. And then say something like:)

Elijah was hiding out. Sometimes we feel like hiding out, too. Doing what God wants us to do is just too hard sometimes. But God sent Elijah an angel who gave him food to sustain him. And God spoke to Elijah. Not in fire. Not in wind. Not with an earthquake, but in a still, small voice that was like a cool breeze. God will sustain us, too. God will give us what we need to do what we are supposed to do.

Closing Music

Use one of the music suggestions or one of your own choosing.

Closing Prayer

Leader: Let's finish with a prayer. God, sometimes we just want to stand out on a cliff and scream, "Louder!" We want to hear you. We want the giant flashing neon arrow to drop out of the sky and point us in the direction you want us to go. But often we already know what it is you are asking of us, and we just don't want to admit it, or we hope you'll change your mind. Sustain us, God. Give us what we need to be your servants. Let us feel your presence. Let us feel your hand on our shoulders. Let us hear your still, small voice. Your servants are listening, God. Amen.

Celebration of Summer Vacation Service

Style Celebratory

Location A large open space with room to dance and jump around or outside where you can feel the warmth of the sun and the play of the breeze throughout the service.

Length 20 to 30 minutes

Materials Lots of string cut into four-foot lengths, one pair of scissors (you keep these), copies of the Order of Worship, Bibles for each reader with their parts marked

Scripture Psalms 25, 30, and 144; Exodus 15:22-27; 1 Corinthians 1:18-2:10

Music Suggestions "Hope" from *Spirit, Draw Near* makes a nice opener for this service. You might try "Fearfully" by Lost and Found from the CD *Pronto*, "Hard Times" by Eastmountainsouth, from their self-titled CD, or "Rusty Cage" from the CD *Unchained* by Johnny Cash. For a final piece, use a classic summer Beach Boys song like "Surfin' USA" or "Fun, Fun, Fun." Both can be found on *The Best of the Beach Boys* CD.

Comments/Ideas Here's a great opportunity to mark an important event in the lives of your students through a unique worship experience.

Introduction

This is a great service to begin summer vacation. It's a celebration of the work and accomplishments of your students in getting through another year of school. (Remember what that was like?)

It's important to let the youth lead this service as much as possible. Let them have ownership of it and re-work it to suit their needs if they desire. Assign a few leaders and let them go. Step in only if you have to. Make copies of the Order of Worship and pass them out so every student has a copy.

Order of Worship

Begin by making sure each person in your group receives three pieces of string. Next have them tie themselves to three different people. There cannot be more than one piece of string connecting any two people. Eventually you will have your whole group tied together as one.

Opening Prayer

God of the seasons, you have given us the summer. You have given us this time when we can feel the sun on our faces and appreciate the refreshing feeling of a gentle breeze. You have given us time to breathe and time to stand getting drenched in the rain. You have given us this planet as a playground, but sometimes we forget that. We have to live by so many rules. We feel trapped by all our plans. Sometimes it feels like our whole lives are already set in stone: We have to study hard, save our money, go to college, get a job, get married, have children. Then maybe we'll have time to do something fun after we retire and before we die. Forgive us for this, God. Forgive us for not understanding we are allowed to play. We are allowed to celebrate. Let us feel the cool, playful breeze of the Holy Spirit as we worship you. Amen.

Music

Choose one of the song suggestions or use one of your own.

Scripture

Exodus 15:22-27; Psalm 25

Responsive Reading

Leader: Anyone who says we need to grow up is already too old.

Group: We deserve a break.

Leader: Anyone who says they remember what it's like to be a teenager doesn't have a clue.

Group: We deserve a break.

Leader: We are young and alive.

Group: We deserve a break.

Leader: School's out for summer.

Group: We deserve a break.

Leader: No more calculators.

No more lockers, locks, or passwords.

No more book bags that weigh as much as we do.

Group: We deserve a break.

Leader: We have studied.

We have worked.

We have stressed out to the point of illness.

Group: We deserve a break.

Leader: We did this so we can be prepared for the so-called real world.

But our parents don't have homework like we do.

Group: We deserve a break.

Leader: We are not yet old. We are not yet dead.

We will celebrate having air in our lungs.

Group: Thank God for summer! *Amen.*

Music

Choose another of the song suggestions or one of your own.

Scripture

1 Corinthians 1:18-2:10; Psalm 30

Responsive Reading

Leader: We are no longer children; we are not yet adults.

Group: We are becoming. God has a plan.

Leader: We are shaped and molded like clay on a potter's wheel.

We have been slammed, smashed, rolled, and cut.

We will eventually go through the fire.

Group: We are becoming. And God will be with us.

Leader: Sometimes it just hurts.

Whatever doesn't kill us will make us stronger.

Group: Whatever holds us down will be broken

when we stand up and dance. *Amen.*

Scripture

Psalm 144

(This psalm was probably written, quite literally, as David was coming out of a dark cave. It should be read loudly.)

Closing Music

During this song produce a pair of scissors and begin setting the students free. Encourage them to move or dance and celebrate being free.

Closing Prayer

God, we are free! Thank you for your blessings of sunshine, wind, music, and friends, for mountains, lightning, oceans, and meadows. Renew us in the days and months ahead. Make us glad for your gift of life. May we experience moments every day when we feel our spirits recharging, moments when we can reevaluate and celebrate the simple pleasures of life. Amen.

What Now? A Post-Easter Service

Style	Prayerful, meditative
Location	Somewhere other than the church building—a parking lot, a roof, a picnic area by a lake, or something like that. If you can't get out of the church, hold the service someplace other than the sanctuary, such as the kitchen.
Length	20 minutes
Materials	Bible, boom box, old candle (see comments), matches, flannel squares (optional—see introduction)
Scripture	Luke 24:13-32; John 21:1-25
Music Suggestions	For opening music, try "Come Thou Fount" by David Crowder Band on the *All I Can Say* CD. There is also a nice version on the disc from The Worship Room. Another option is "Superman" by Five For Fighting off the *America Town* CD. Options for closing music include "Baby" on the *This* CD by Lost and Found or "Fruit We Bear" from the group's *Something* CD. You can use "Fields of Gold" performed by Sting; there's also a really nice version of the same song on the Eva Cassidy album *Songbird*. If you are feeling really experimental, try Johnny Cash's version of "Personal Jesus" on the *American IV* CD. Try working in "And Death Willl Have No Dominion" from the *Spirit, Draw Near* CD.
Comments/Ideas	Since this service is about Christ's ongoing presence, don't use a brand new candle. Instead, find one that's left over from an old Advent wreath. The more beat-up the candle looks, the better. Don't forget matches.

Introduction

Jesus is here, *now*. Jesus himself said, "I am with you always." The goal of this service is to help the youth understand the story of Christ did not end on Easter morning. It's still going on.

To give your service a tactile sense, you may want to buy some old baby blankets or flannel pajamas at your local thrift store. Wash these in a baby detergent and fabric softener and cut them into small squares. These will be passed out at the beginning of the service and are intended to emphasize the feeling of *security* we get when we know Jesus is with us no matter what.

Order of Worship

Leader: The story of Jesus does not stop at the resurrection. The Gospels keep going with stories about how Jesus continued to appear to the disciples again and again. The Gospel of John even says, "Jesus did many other things that are not recorded in this book." Jesus kept coming back to let his disciples know he was going to be with them forever.

Jesus appeared to two of the disciples as they were walking along the road. That's why we are out here. We're on the road inviting Jesus to be among us.

I'm going to hand you something. *(Pass out the swatches of flannel.)* Hold this in your hand, running it back and forth in your fingers as we worship. Let it remind you of the security of a child's blanket, a comforting presence available in every moment.

Opening Prayer

All: Creator God, the Easter eggs are mostly gone. We've grown tired of plastic grass and pastel-colored candy. The chocolate bunnies and marshmallow peeps have lost their appeal, and we sort of feel let down. The resurrection of your Son is a celebration. But now, like the disciples, we wonder: What's next? Help us to see that the celebration does not end, God. Come into our worship and make your presence known as we try to get closer to your Son. Amen.

Opening Music

Play the selection you have chosen.

Scripture

Luke 24:13-32

Leader: The Scripture says the two on the Emmaus road that day were kept from recognizing Jesus. The Bible doesn't say whether this was some supernatural thing Jesus the Miracle Worker did to them, or if he simply covered his head with his cloak, or if they were just too distraught to see who was with them. We do know they certainly wouldn't have been expecting him to show up and walk with them! Jesus was right there next to them, and they didn't see him. Sometimes we do the same.

Responsive Reading

Leader: When the blind were made to see,

Group: Jesus was there.

Leader: When the broken stood and walked,

Group: Jesus was there.

Leader: When the wandering found a path to follow,

Group: Jesus was there.

Leader: When Mary and the women went to the tomb,

Group: Jesus was there.

Leader: When the eleven gathered in the room,

Group: Jesus was there.

Leader: When the disciples walked along the road,

Group: Jesus was there.

Scripture

John 21:1-25

This is a great passage. Remember in Matthew's gospel, Peter was the one who, in response to his own faith, had walked on the water? Now in this story, also in response to his faith, he jumps into the water again—and this time he swims to shore. Can you imagine how happy you would be if some-one who had died, someone whom you loved dearly, appeared suddenly to you—calling to you from a long way off? Would you believe? Or would you question your own eyes?

Responsive Reading

Leader: When the disciples tried to return to their jobs,

Group: Jesus was there.

Leader: When Thomas doubted,

Group: Jesus was there.

Leader: When the disciples ate their breakfast,

Group: Jesus was there.

Leader: When Peter wondered what was next,

Group: Jesus was there.

Leader: Jesus did not appear to the disciples on a flaming chariot, in a flash of light, or in some other spectacular way. He came to them in the most simple, everyday moments: as they walked along the road, as they did their jobs, as they ate a meal. Mark's gospel

says the risen Jesus was in "another form." This is still true. Jesus appears today in another form: in us, as the body of Christ.

Responsive Reading

Leader: When a child is born.

Group: Jesus *IS* there.

Leader: When the hungry are fed,

Group: Jesus *IS* there.

Leader: When we gather in his name,

Group: Jesus *IS* there.

Leader: When we celebrate Easter,

Group: Jesus *IS* there.

Leader: When we clean up the mess afterward,

Group: Jesus *IS* there.

Leader: When we stand in the (kitchen, rest stop, parking lot) and read the Scriptures,

Group: Jesus *IS* there.

Leader: When we go to school,

Group: Jesus *IS* there.

Leader: When we talk with our friends,

Group: Jesus *IS* there.

Leader: When we live our lives,

Group: Jesus *IS* there.

Closing Music

Play the selection you've chosen.

Closing Prayer

Living God, you sent your Son into this world, and for some reason, we think it's a story with a happy ending. The truth is, the story does not end. It continued through the lives of the disciples and through the early church. The story went on through the Middle Ages and into the Reformation. And it continues now: right here in *this* moment. Jesus is alive—and lives and breathes as we live and breathe. Give us the eyes to see the risen Jesus in one another. Help us to live as the body of Christ. Thank you, God, for allowing us to be a part of you through the life and continued presence of your Son, our Savior, Jesus Christ. Amen.

A Road Trip Service

Style	Contemplative, praiseful, rejuvenating
Location	Any highway rest stop or large parking lot along your road trip
Length	15 to 20 minutes
Materials	Communion elements, stuff you find in the parking lot, boom box, Bible
Scripture	Psalm 121; Acts 27:13-28:10
Music Suggestions	Because you are building an altar out of refuse and other materials in a roadside parking lot, it's a nice twist to play some high church music. For the first song, try something from Chanticleer off the *Magnificat* CD. Jeff Johnson has some nice selections on the *Vespers* CD. "Table of Christ" from *Spirit, Draw Near* is excellent. If you prefer something that matches the mood of an outdoor, rest-stop altar, try using the *Speedwood Hymns* CD from Lost and Found. If you are brave, use "Boulevard of Broken Dreams" off of Green Day's *American Idiot* CD. (It has one curse word, and it's a biggie.) If you use this tune as an opening, be sure to find something uplifting to close the service.
Comments/Ideas	This is a great impromptu service to hold around midweek of a mission trip or halfway through a very long drive.

Introduction

Before you begin this service, you will need to build an altar. Tell the youth the men and women of Scripture would sometimes build a makeshift altar using whatever they might find in the place where they were. Often they used rocks and other objects to mark places where they had experienced God's presence. Send your youth out in groups of two or three and have them bring back whatever they can find to build a worship area.

Order of Worship

Opening Prayer

Leader: Ever-present God, stay with us. Surround us as we travel. Whether we are lost, or stuck in traffic, or cruising right along, help us to know you are with us. Give us patience and kindness. Strengthen us with energy and endurance. Help us to embrace this opportunity to grow together as a group. Give us time to share junk

food and weird stories. We are riding across your creation. Help us remember that the world you love is outside the window and also inside the car. Amen.

Music

Play one of the suggested pieces or choose one of your own.

Stories of the Road

Leader: When Moses led the people out of Egypt, they had been held captive there for years. Most of them had never been beyond the city walls. Most of them probably had no knowledge of anything beyond the city where they were slaves. But they spent the next 40 years on the road. And at one point, Moses got some of his artists together, and they built a worship space they could carry with them as they traveled.

Later when Joshua led the Israelites across the Jordan River, God told them to take 12 stones and build an altar. And so they built an altar using the stones they found in that place, as a symbol of God's presence with them.

There's a great Bible passage that we can imagine Moses or Joshua might have used when he stopped with his group to worship and thank God.

Scripture 1

Psalm 121

Responsive Reading

Leader: We are on a mission from God.

Group: Show us the way.

Leader: We are stopping for a moment of rest.

Group: Show us the way.

Leader: God is here. God is with us.

Group: Show us the way.

Leader: When we get back on the road,

Group: Show us the way.

Leader: When we take the wrong exit,

Group: Show us the way.

Leader: When we can't find a way to get along,

Group: Show us the way.

Leader: Your Son said he was the way.

Group: Show us the way.

Leader: Your Son called us to follow him.

Group: Show us the way.

Leader: You are not only our destination.

Group: Show us the way.

Leader: You are our traveling companion.

Group: Show us the way.

Leader: Be our compass, God.

Group: Show us the way.

All: Amen.

Leader: Now, I'm going to read you a story from the book of Acts. It's about a road trip. Notice absolutely nothing got in the way of Paul's doing what God had called him to do.

Scripture 2

Acts 27:13-28:10

Communion

Leader: The last time Jesus was able to gather with his friends for a meal was the night he was arrested. Jesus had to know what was coming when he sat down to celebrate the Passover with them. That would be like you having Thanksgiving dinner knowing the cops were on the way to arrest you, and you were never going to see your friends and family again. So Jesus used what was available to him to let his friends know he would never forget them, and they should never forget him.

He took some bread, and he broke it. He gave it to them. They all took some. He said, "Take. Eat. This is my body."

(Pass the bread around.)

Then he poured the wine in a cup, and he handed it to each of them. He said, "Take. Drink. This is my blood."

(Pass the juice around.)

After a celebratory meal in Jesus' time, worshipers would sing together to praise God. That's how we're going to close this service before we load it back up and keep moving.

Music

Play one of the suggested pieces or come up with your own.

Closing Prayer

God, we are going to load it up again and move on. We need to feel your presence. We are here as your servants, and like Moses, Ruth, Isaiah, and Mary, we will go where we are sent. We are not complaining about the destination, loving God. We just want to know we are on the right path. Surround us. Rejuvenate us. Uplift us. Strengthen us. Hold us. Amen.

Blessings

Here's a collection of brief blessings that you or a member of your youth group can lead. A blessing is a short (usually) prayer that invokes the Spirit of God to be present in a person, place, or thing in a very real way. It's not about confession or forgiveness; it's used to ask God to grant special favor. Gather whatever youth you have with you. If appropriate, place your hand on the person or item to be blessed (this is especially effective if all your youth do the same) and read the blessing. Everyone should join in on "Amen."

Baby

God, bless this new addition to the world. Make (her, him) strong, healthy, and wise. May (she, he) know love and understanding all (her, his) days. Thank you for the gift that is __(baby's name)__, and let the light that shines from (her, him) illuminate us all. Amen.

Bakeries

The blessings of God are as sweet to us as the air in this bakery. Bless this place, God, and all who work here. May the Lord who multiplied the loaves and fishes make your bread rise, your frosting smooth, and your customers content. Amen.

Bus Drivers

God, thank you for your servant in whom we have entrusted our lives. Give (him, her) smooth roads, light traffic, no annoying drivers with cell phones, and abiding peace. Give (him, her) comfort in (his, her) chair and ease in (his, her) shoulders. Bless the hands and the knowledge that move this rolling fortress safely down the highway. Amen.

Cab Drivers

May the God of all journeys clear a path for you. May your lane be free of potholes. May your passengers be kind and generous. May your tips be large and your sense of direction certain. May God keep you safe and restore you when you are weary. Amen.

Campsite

God of the wilderness, you have created this world and allowed us to borrow it for a time. Let us use your creation respectfully. Bless this place, and let all that happens in this campsite glorify you. May we leave this place better than it was when we got here. May *we* leave this place better than *we* were when we got here. Amen.

Church

God, may this place truly be a sanctuary. May all who come here find peace. May all who come here find inspiration. May all who come here find you. Let this church be like your own arms—open to receive the lost and the wandering in an embrace of your love. Amen.

College-Bound Students

Every journey has multiple beginnings and endings. Every step is something new. May God send angels to guide you on this next step. May the Lord bless and reward your decision to become a better servant by challenging you to be a better person. May the halls of higher education receive you, stretch you, enlighten you, and make you ready for the next journey. Amen.

Construction Workers

In a world accomplished at knocking things down, may God bless your ability to build. May all your lines be true. May all your nails be straight. May the supplies never run out. May your clients never change their minds. May the angels of heaven give rest to your hands, back, and feet. May God bless and keep safe those who will work and live in your creation. Amen.

Cooks

May God make your kitchen an orchestra. May the angels of heaven come and sing around your stove. May all the pots, pans, and ingredients be your instruments. May the food you create here be your symphony. Let all those who eat the food you have prepared glorify the God who gives us all we need. Amen.

Dancers

May your dancing lead you into joy. May you know your body as a magnificent instrument, a gift from God. May you soar into the heights of gratitude as you bend, twist, spin, and become airborne. With every stretch, celebrate that you belong to God. May you dance as King David danced—without shame or worry, and fully aware you are dancing for God...only for God. Amen.

Diner

May this be a place where people experience God speaking gently to them, saying, "Come to me, and I will give you rest." May all those who come through the door find rest, may they find company, may they find warmth, and may they find peace. May your tables be clean, your napkin supply endless, your food a pleasure, and your customers kings. Amen.

Doctors

Healing God, bless the hands of this servant of yours. Thank you for (his, her) mind and the eyes that can see what others cannot. Thank you for (his, her) strength and perseverance. Make (him, her) more than a physician;

make (him, her) a healer of your children. Guide (his, her) hands. Guide (his, her) thoughts. And where (he, she) may suffer, God, make (him, her) whole. Amen.

Fast-Food Workers

May God bless you as a servant of God's people. May the customers not complain but treat you with the respect you so deserve. May the children not use ketchup as a toy. May you see smiles and not frowns. May the lunch rush be kind. May God keep reserved in your name a special table in God's five-star restaurant. Amen.

Gardens

May the God of all things green sustain your garden and rain down love, peace, and joy on all who look upon it. May this bit of earth produce in abundance all things planted here. May any harmful bugs stay off your leaves, and every flower, fruit, and vegetable reach its due season. And may this garden and its gardener grow and face the sun. Amen.

Graduates

God, there is a low rumble here. Like a drum roll. Like thunder. Like a fuse. There is a sense something big is just on the horizon. Dance in the hearts, minds, and souls of these graduates, ever-creating God, as they mark this ending and race forward into new beginnings. Let this graduation, this symphony, this storm, this explosion, be heard in heaven. Amen.

Grandparents

May the wisdom and experience you have in your eyes be passed down to those whose lives are just beginning. May you see all the generations of the past in the one in front of you. May you live your life knowing your presence matters here. May the God who laughs like a child fill your heart. Amen.

Homemakers

God, home is where the heart is. Home is where love is. Home is where you are. Bless all those people who have made the choice to be makers of homes. Let them create a sanctuary of safety, comfort, and peace of mind. May the laundry load be light, the counters clean, and the supper always unburned. May all who benefit from their work show their appreciation. And may they find respite when their bodies and souls grow tired. Amen.

Hospital Workers

God of healing, there are those who work the system and those who make the system work. Each and every part of this hospital is invaluable. No part can function without the other. All the workers here, no matter their job, are healers. Let their words and their hands help create a place where your creations can become well. Amen.

Hospitalized Youth

God of joy, let your presence be known in this room. Let your Spirit hover over this bed and give strength and healing to its occupant. Let the doctors and nurses and interns and custodians all do their jobs so __(youth's name)__ can do (his, hers) and become well. Let your touch speed the healing and take away the pain. Give (him, her) comfort and rest and peace. Amen.

Hotel Workers

God of the unsung, just as you carried, as if on the wings of eagles, the bone-weary Israelites out of the land of Egypt, so may you lift up the spirits of those who come in to clean this room after us. May their corners be smooth and their floors be clean. May you fill them with pride in hard work well done. May their compensation and tips be fair and generous. May they find in you all they need in life. And at the end of their days, may you reserve the penthouse suite for them and let the angels wait on their every whim. Amen.

Mail Carriers

God of angels, send your messengers down to hover around this messenger on (his, her) appointed rounds. (He, she) brings news as your angels brought news: news of births, bills, and blessings; news of hope, friendship, and love. Keep the rain off (his, her) head and the dogs off (his, her) feet. Let the traffic be light and the recipients be kind. Give strength to (his, her) back and swiftness to (his, her) feet. Amen.

Mission Trip Blessings
Before Departing

Guiding and loving God, go with these people, these servants, these members of our church who seek by their actions to show the world your love. Protect them, teach them, and support them as they take this next step in their own journeys to becoming the people you want them to be. Amen.

House Blessing

May the Holy Spirit of God fill this house with joy and laughter. May all those who come through this door receive God's peace. May the walls keep out the cold wind and the door keep out the cold hearts. Be warm. Be safe. Be at home. Amen.

Work Blessing

God, look down on the work we do this week and bless the hands that do it. May the paint go far, the nails go in straight, and the gardens bring forth abundance. Bless these workers, God. May we feel your presence even when we are tired and aching. May your love refresh us like a glass of cold lemonade. May we be able to do what we came to do. Amen.

Blessing of the People

God of compassion, as we go from this place, may your presence stay here. May you be in these walls, these floors, and in every breath of air both inside and outside this house. Most of all, God, be in these people and let them know you all their days. Amen.

After Returning

Receiving and welcoming God, we have returned home from your service. Your servants are tired but changed, weary but not dejected, exhausted but renewed.

These are your servants, God. Thank you for them. Thank you for what they have done. They have gone into the world and taken the love of your Son Jesus Christ and held it up with their actions and their attitudes. We welcome them home. May they look for continuing opportunities to serve you in the mission fields that surround them every day. Amen.

Musicians

God, you announced the arrival of your Son with the songs of angels. Your greatest king, David, composed songs and soothed souls with the music of his lyre. Reveal yourself to and through these musicians. Inspire their music to lift, to teach, to love, and to heal. Amen.

New Church

God of wonders, we are growing. We have left the old building behind like we leave behind a wonderful pair of comfortable shoes. No matter how good it felt to slip into them, we always knew we could not wear them forever. Thank you, God, for this new place. And now, may your Word be heard anew here. May your Spirit be felt afresh. May those in the world who are aching to find sanctuary find it here. May your name be praised until the end of days. Amen.

New Church Van

God, make this your chariot. Let us go to and from all the places we go with the assurance that you are present with us. Watch over us as we travel in this van. Let the laughter and singing and sleeping and eating and discussing that happen in this van be pleasing to you. Amen.

New Pastor

God, thank you for sending us your servant __(pastor's name)__. Bless (her, him). Hold (her, him) close. Support (her, him) as (she, he) begins (her, his) service here. Keep the complainers to a minimum. Keep the people awake on Sunday mornings. Keep (her, him) away from the yellow stuff at the potluck suppers. Let (her, him) grow and serve and become whom you have called (her, him) to be, and let (her, him) do it here. Amen.

New School Year

God of learning, it's like making footprints on new snow. It's like seeing grass after living at the North Pole for a year. There is so much promise in this day. There is so much possibility. There are amazing things that can happen this year. May we soar into this year with our heads high. May our entrance into the new year be as bold as football players bursting through the hoop of paper. We've been doing this a long time. But this year is a whole new chance. Bless us, and help us make the most of it. Amen.

New Youth Minister

God, thank you for bringing __(minister's name)__ into this bizarre group of people. (He, She) has no idea what (he, she) is in for. Brace (him, her), God. Put your hand on (his, her) shoulder and try not to laugh (or teach us all when we ought to laugh!). Let (him, her) step into this with (his, her) eyes wide open. If (he, she) goes screaming into the night, let (him, her) come back. If (he, she) gets to know us and decides (he, she) wants to go pump gasoline or flip burgers, well, we understand. We will take it easy for a little while, God. (He, she) is your servant and may have something to teach us that we don't already know. We will welcome (him, her) without comparing (him, her) to the one who just left. That's not fair. We will make (him, her) a part of this group. We will celebrate (him, her) as a gift from you. Amen.

New Youth Room

God, thank you for this space. It is our space. It is where we will gather together and be in your presence. Someday, when we are as old as _____ (youth director), may we remember this as the place where you made yourself known to us. May we remember this as the place where we understood you were more than a word in a prayer. May this place be as our own sanctuary, where we can be who and what we truly are and feel safe to become what we want to become. Thank you for this space, God. May we always use it to serve your purposes.

Nurses

God, you have put angels on this earth in the form of nurses. You have given them the ability to heal. They are our friends, our therapists, our family, and our support group. Give them inspiration when they don't feel inspired. Give them energy when they have none. Give them patience with their patients. Above all else, God, let them know your Spirit's presence. Work through them, through their hands and voices and eyes and ears and hearts. Amen.

Prom Night

God of the night sky, let your stars shine for these young people. Let them hear music and dance close and smell like perfume and aftershave. Let this night be special for them. Keep them safe. Keep them smart. Keep them in your watchful eye, and let them celebrate this night as one more joyous step into their own lives. Amen.

Restaurant Server

May God bring peace to your mind, lightness to your feet, and strength to your arms and back. May you have big tippers, quiet children, and customers who don't complain. May your smile brighten the day of those you serve and their smiles in return brighten yours. And may you always know God has a place for you in heaven with big, comfortable chairs and angels waiting to take your order. Amen.

Road Trip

God of the open highway, go with us now as we embark on an amazing journey. Let us be fueled by caffeine and loud music. Let us enjoy every moment of this trip. Let us learn, talk, rest, and laugh. Let us play silly games and buy tacky souvenirs. Bring us closer to each other, and bring us closer to you. Guide us as we journey. Amen.

School Employees

God, most teachers don't have a degree in education. There are teachers in the office, on the bus, in the cafeteria. Bless them all, God. Bless those who clean up after we leave and those who show up before the first teacher arrives. Bless those who must clean bizarre stains, dole out medications, and keep every file, pencil, pen, and phone log in order. Let them all remember they are ALL teachers. They work with your children, loving God; let them all teach. Amen.

Shelter Workers

God, these people are your hands. They are in daily contact with your Son. They feed the hungry, warm the cold, shelter those who have no roof, and companion the lonely. God, these people are what you meant when you said, "Take care of each other." If everyone, from the street sweepers to the politicians, were just to follow their example, there would be no more hungry, cold, or lonely people on your earth. Save a mansion in heaven for them, God. Amen.

Surgeons

God, bless and guide the hands of this physician. We know it is your power working through (her, him). (She, He) heals as you healed. Help (her, him) to make (her, his) patients whole again. Work in (her, his) heart. Work in (her, his) mind. Work in (her, his) hands. Let (her, him) use the knowledge (she, he) has learned, and let (her, him) call on the experience (she, he) has gathered. Let (her, him) be your tool of healing. Amen.

Teachers

God of learning, these people should be working in palaces and making seven-figure salaries. They are not. They are here in this place, doing this work, because they love your children. They have a gift of imparting knowledge. Let them be like waterfalls and their students like sponges. Guide and protect them. Strengthen and uplift them. Give them grace. Amen.

Prayers

In this section, you'll find nearly 200 prayers on a wide variety of topics. These prayers are written to work equally well when led by a youth leader or when spoken by the youth in unison. The prayers can be used on their own exactly as written, adapted to better fit your situation, or incorporated into any of the worship services in either volume of *The Book of Uncommon Prayer*. Use the words and ideas here to spark your own prayers with youth.

Acceptance

Of God's Will

God, you are in charge—and we are not. Help us get that through our thick skulls. Forgive us when we demand you change our lives and fix our problems. Help us accept there are some things we cannot change. Sometimes we beat our heads against a wall until we are bloodied. This is not healthy, God. We do not help ourselves when we push against a door that says "Pull." Help us take a step back. Help us take a deep breath and accept those things we may not like which you may have put in our lives for a reason. We will wait. We will be patient. Amen.

Of Others

God, if only everyone were like me, it would be so much easier. If only everyone were like us, it would be so much easier. Why did you make people so different? How are we supposed to know who is on our side and who isn't? You told us to love one another, but could you make it a little easier? We will accept one another, God. We know we are not perfect, and we will stop demanding others measure up to the standards we set for them. Help us to love one another just as you have loved us. Amen.

{ 84 }

Accountability

God, you made the rain, the snow, the stars, the sun, the moon, the mountains, and the ants. Sometimes we seem to forget you are God, and we are not. Yet we know you have given us responsibility in your world. Help us take responsibility for the things put under our care. Help us own up to the problems we create for others and ourselves. It's easy for us to point fingers and place blame when things go wrong. When we mess up, help us admit it to ourselves and others. When we are part of a job well done, help us share the kudos with others who shared in the process. Help us get over ourselves, God. Once we understand you are God and we are not, that sort of thing becomes easier. Send us a reminder, God. Just don't let it hurt too much. Amen.

Accountants (Numbers People)

God of numbers, thank you for creating all kinds of people and putting them all over this earth. Your creation is full of so many mysteries. Thank you for the people who can see order in the chaos. Thank you for the people who can see the patterns and possibilities. Thank you for those who can see method in music. Thank you for the theorist theologians. Some of us can't count past 10 without removing our shoes. Some of us are still trying to figure out why someone put letters in with the numbers. You made all kinds of people, God. Thank you for those who can see the potential and help us understand this universe you created. Amen.

Achievement

We did it, God. We knew we could. There were those who said it would never happen, but we did it. And we know what we have achieved was possible only because you made it possible. We can do all things through you. We can overcome obstacles through you. We can see the goals through you. This was a long time coming, God, and we worked so hard. Thank you for being there every step of the way. Thank you for never letting us get too discouraged. Thank you for raising our spirits, for granting us patience, and for putting up with our attitudes. We did something amazing here, God. Thank you. Amen.

Advent

Father God, it is too easy to be cynical. It is too easy to believe Christmas is too commercial, the stores are ripping us off, and the lyrics to our favorite Christmas songs are just words. We need faith, Lord. We need the faith to believe we can make a difference, faith that you are there and you are listening, faith that "all is calm" and "all is bright." We need the unyielding faith of a child, Lord. We need to understand there was a reason you came to Earth as an infant. Give us the faith of a child, Lord. Amen.

Advent (Candlelight)

Father in heaven, let the light of this candle be the light that leads us home. Too often we feel like we are left in the dark—alone and cold. We know you gave us your Son as a light in our darkness. But this candle is just one light, Lord, and it's a big world. Help us carry that light for you. Renew us in this time of year when things seem so crazy. When we are at the mall or the post office, help us remember that the true reason for the celebration is the light you have brought into our world and into our lives, the light of Jesus Christ our Lord. Amen.

Addiction

God, few of us understand addiction. We may make jokes about it, or we put on our concerned faces—but we don't get it. Remind us that our lack of understanding is okay, but it doesn't make the problem any less real. God, help those who struggle with addictions today. Give us patience, kindness, compassion, love, and a willingness to stand by those who need us. Overcoming a serious addiction is one of the hardest experiences a person can go through. Sticking with someone through that struggle can be nearly as hard. Give us the strength and assurance you are there with us. Amen.

All Hallows' Eve

God, we can't even begin to imagine what it will be like to live in your house. The best we have down here doesn't even begin to approach the paradise you have planned for us. Help us not to fear death so much. Give us the faith to believe death is not something evil, but instead a doorway to a place where there is no pain, no sadness, no fear, and no hatred. Death brings us to a place so overwhelmingly wonderful that if we were to experience just a blink of it here, we would be lifted right off the ground. We know your Son Jesus will stand at the door and meet us with open arms. We will walk into the embrace of Christ, and we will be new. Amen.

Creator God, forgive us our impatience. We want to know what's going on all the time. We are afraid of the unknown—and death is the biggest unknown of all. That is why we fear it. Sometimes we get angry with you because we don't understand. You see the completed puzzle. We can see just one small piece. Have patience with us. Don't be too angry with us, God. Instead give us faith. Give us strength. Help us laugh and be joyful for those who have already gone to your home. Let us be happy for them. Amen.

Angels

God, Creator of angels, we have all kinds of pictures in our heads of what your messengers look like. We've seen them in movies and in the breakables section of the Christian bookstore. If these images are all we have, then let that be enough. We know you will make your message known to us, if we are meant to hear it. Send your angels now, God. Send angels of peace, love, harmony, strength, and protection. Surround us with your beings of light, and let us feel your presence through them. Amen.

God, your cherubim and seraphim are here. Let us hear them praise you, so we can join in the song. Let us feel their influence on our path and our patience. Open our ears to hear them whisper that you love us, even when we feel unlovable. Make us your servants. Send us to do your work, to preach your Word. Make us your angels, God. We are listening. Tell us what to do. Amen.

Anger

At God

God, where were you? Why am I alone down here? I do everything I'm told. I believe in your promises. I tell others you love every one of us. And lately all I get from you is silence. The only answer I get to my prayers is "no." I'm not selfish, God. I'm a good person. I have faith—but when I asked you for help, you turned me down. You flat-out ignored me and the pain

I was going through. You left me high and dry, but you still expect me to love you? How am I supposed to do that? I'm not asking you to rain down money on my life—but lately it feels like you are stepping on it! I'm done talking. I need to be silent for a while. Amen.

At Others

God of perfection, why do you insist on letting the idiots run the show? Why are some people so foolish? Sometimes I have such a desire to knock heads together that I can't stop my hands from shaking! I don't need to get my own way all the time, but would it kill you to help me out once in a while? They say you look after the fools—and I'm glad that's true. But sometimes I think if you hadn't made so many fools, you might have time left over to make things run a little smoother down here for all of us. I'm glad you gave us patience, because I'm gonna need it. And if you have any extra sitting around...could you send it my way? Please? Amen.

At Ourselves

God, help me to keep my mouth shut sometimes. I get in these moods, and suddenly I'm mouthing off and hurting those I most love and care about. I do things I know are wrong and make a mess of my life; then I seem to look for what I can do to make a mess of others' lives, too! And the worst part is, I knew this would happen—I knew when I chose to go down this path, I would wind up hurting someone. And now, here I am. I could kick myself, God, and I deserve whatever you are going to send to me. But I ask you to send me a little peace, please, Father. Blow a gentle breeze my way. Cool my burning head and thoughts. Calm me. Soothe me. Then give me strength to do what I can to fix the mess I've made. Amen.

Anxiety

Did you make stress, God? Was it one of your creations—or one of ours? If you made us, doesn't that mean you are partly responsible? Do you have any idea what my normal day is like? Have you been down here lately? Everybody wants everything from me. Six people call my name at once, and five get mad if I don't respond to them first. I have so much going on—sometimes I wish I could walk away from my life! But where would I go? The same insanity is waiting for me anywhere I go. I need a moment's peace, God. I need a day off. I need just a hint of that everlasting joy you've promised. Can you share some of it? Just a little? Amen.

Appearances

God, help me stop comparing myself with the beautiful people. Why do I put such a high priority on looking like the people I see on magazine covers and TV shows? Why do I judge myself—and others—based on clothing and hairstyles? I am so much more than that, God. Help me see the beauty in others, so others can see it in me. I am not a pretty picture with a personality as flat as the paper it's printed on. I am so much more. Help me to live my life as "more than that." Help me show the world that my light, my beauty, and my worth come from my soul and not my sense of fashion. Amen.

Artists

God, there are those who think so far outside the box that they don't even know where "the box" is anymore. Some of us see the colored leaves on a tree; others focus on the black trunk. But then there are others who see the tree and imagine forests and squirrels and mice and gnats and campfires and forest fires and sap and streams and birds and beasts. They can't help it, God. It's the way you wired them. Thank you for the artists, God. When the rest of the room is taking notes, they are drawing portraits and comic books. Bless those whose creative minds carry them a thousand miles away—and give us the patience to see the visions you have shared with them. You are the greatest Creator, O God. You created the colors. Let our artists see them all, and give them courage to be who they are, even when the world doesn't understand. Amen.

{ 88 } Atheists

Thank you for the faith that comes as a gift from you, O God. We have felt your presence, and we believe in you. But there are others who have not made a decision to follow you, and they may argue and get angry with those of us who believe. We don't have proof for them, God. You don't work that way. We don't have evidence that will remove their every doubt. But we know we have met you, God. And someday they will see you. Someday you will put your face down close beside theirs, and they will see you. Take care of them, Father, for we know they are your children. Guide their feet on the path that leads them, and us, back to you. Amen.

Athletes

God of movement, there is grace in sport. Thank you for giving us physical bodies that allow us to do amazing things. Thank you for the thrill of competition and achievement. Thank you for games that demand we be a horse and, at the same time, a bird. We know there are those whom you have blessed with remarkable skills, strength, agility, speed, strategy, and competitive souls. Bless those who are always trying to do better, always reaching for the next goal. Bless those who drive themselves forward when it's often so much easier to sit back and quit. You created athletes of all kinds, sizes, and abilities. Help us keep our eyes on the prize, God. Amen.

Authority

You are God. We are not. Help us start there. God, we don't like to be told what to do, but we know you have placed some persons in positions of authority. Help us see authority as a voice of experience and wisdom. Help us see those in charge as people who have our best interests at heart. Help us understand we don't have to question every word that comes out of someone's mouth just because that person is in authority! We have questioned you, God. We have stood on the mountain and said, "Why?" Help us remember that sometimes "because I said so" is answer enough. Forgive us for our presumptuousness, God. We know you are in charge. You see the big picture in a way we can't. Help us learn to follow you more closely and live as you have taught us. Amen.

Autumn

God, we see the cycle of the seasons. Summer ends and runs into fall, which gives way to winter, and then spring. Autumn is a season of change—and it reminds us we are changing, too. Things we used to need we may need no longer. Help us throw off those things that hold us down, so we might become something new. This is a time when there is an explosion of color, and then it starts to get cold again. This is part of life. Help us understand we cannot live in summer forever. We cannot be growing like a garden in the spring all the time. We are made to change, and this season is part of it. Let us welcome the change. Let us see the beauty of your earth as it prepares to sleep in the wintertime. Let us embrace this time of change and become something new. Amen.

Babies

New in the Family

Father God, you have put a new life on this planet. You have taken all the potential in the universe and dropped it into our presence here and now. Everything this child is now is what we once were. You have given us this new life and charged us with a great responsibility. You knew this child long before (he, she) arrived here, just as you knew each of us long before we were born. This life is just a moment in time, but right now there is so much of it. How can one being so small bring so much light into the world? We are all big brothers and sisters, God. We are protectors and teachers. Help us. Amen.

Sick

God, take this, your smallest servant, into your healing arms. Let this child feel the beat of your heart, the nearness of you. We feel so helpless, God. Hands so small should not have to carry such a burden. Bless the doctors, nurses, and all those who are trained to heal. Bless the parents and other relatives who care for and worry over this tiniest family member. Bless this child, God, for (she, he) is just beginning this journey. We remember you sent your Son as a baby into this world for us. Let this baby grow bigger and stronger so (she, he) will have a chance to change your world by changing our lives. Amen.

Backbiting/Backstabbing

God of compassion, we are all your children. You have made every one of us in your own image. But sometimes we act like we've forgotten this. Why must we be so insecure about ourselves that we put each other down in order to feel like we belong? Your Son said, as we treat others, so have we treated him. Forgive us for ignoring your Son, God. Forgive us for excluding him from our lives. Forgive us for going out of our way to make him feel small. That's not who we are. That's not who you want us to be. Forgive us. Amen.

God, sometimes we want to keep our circle of friends tight and small. We don't want others included. We say things that hurt, God. We say things about one another that are meant to exclude. That's not how you made us. You made us as one people. You made us and brought us together—and we have the choice of either cherishing one another or hurting one another. Sometimes we make the wrong choice, God. What's worse is each of us knows what it feels like to be excluded, and yet we see no problem in shutting out others whom you've created. Help us let go of the hands that keep people out. Help us let people in so our circle encompasses the world. Amen.

Bad Moods

God, whatever it is we need to get us through this day...please give it to us. We love one another—but if we have to keep spending time together, you may see one or more of us more quickly than you planned! We need rest. We need peace of mind. We need to be heard. We are frustrated, and we're taking it out on one another. Give us laughter, God. Give us patience. Show us again the reason we enjoy being together. We need you on this one, God. You gave us one another; now help us tolerate one another. Help us love one another. Make us your children. Amen.

Balance

God, we need the darkness in order to appreciate the light. We need silence so we can enjoy the sound. We need laughter because we have so many tears. Our lives are so out of balance, God. We have too much of one thing and not enough of another. This is our own fault. We fill our lives with worthless things that throw off our balance. When one person jumps off the seesaw, disaster happens. Life out of balance is a path to destruction. Give us what we need. Help us take on the burdens others are carrying so we may walk along together. Help us share all we have so no one is hungry, hurting, grieving, lost, or alone. Amen.

Boldness

God of light, you did not fill the earth with boring colors. You did not create a world of music and sound so we could live with our hands over our ears. Help us live out of the shadows. Help us live at full volume. Help us live wide open to the possibilities. This world has so much to offer, but we cannot appreciate it if we never leave the corner. Give us the courage to try, the courage to fail, and the courage to get up again if we fall. Help us to live boldly. A light under a bowl does no one any good. Salt that has lost its flavor is of no value. Life lived under a table isn't living. God of the senses, give us flavor, give us light, and give us life. Amen.

Boredom

God, life is a celebration. We should never be bored. Each moment, each breath, each day is a gift from you. Of all the things we have created to complicate our lives, boredom is the most useless. We need only look into the night sky and remember that each star is a sun with planets revolving around it, and if we stood on one of those planets, we'd see more stars. We need only consider the inner workings of a flower, a field of grass, or the human body to appreciate what you have done. We don't need a telescope or a microscope to see we are the wondrous creations of a wondrous Creator. Life is not boring unless we make it so. We will get out of our lives exactly what we put into them. Amen.

Prayers

Breakfast Prayers

Casual

God of morning, sometimes the light that comes through the window hurts our eyes. Thank you for the day. Sometimes the floor is cold when we pull back the blankets. Thank you for our feet. Sometimes breakfast is eaten out of a paper bag or a foil packet. Thank you for Pop-Tarts and doughnuts. Forgive us if we grumble, God. There are those who have less than we do. This small breakfast would be a banquet in some places. We thank you for food. We thank you for coffee. We thank you for juice. Mostly we thank you for one another and this opportunity to be together. Each day is a gift from you. We may not realize it now, but it is. We will celebrate—just as soon as we've had something to eat. Amen.

Fancy

God of pancakes and strawberries, we stand around this table, and the good smells are evidence you exist. Coffee, juice, doughnuts, fruits, sausage, biscuits, milk—it's all good, and it's all from you. This is how we celebrate life. This is how we celebrate the new dawn. This is how we celebrate the gifts you have given us. Each day is new. Let us gather here to laugh and talk and refuel, so we may face the joys and challenges of this day you have given us. Give us this moment of peace and connection, and then be with us as we go. Bless this good food and the hands that prepared it. Amen.

Broken Homes

God of love, nobody lives in a perfect TV world. We don't all have happy households where everyone gets along and every problem gets resolved in 30 minutes with commercials. We live in the real world, God. "Honor thy father and mother" doesn't work when thy father and mother can't stand each other. Sometimes we just have to ride it out, God. I can't pray for you to fix it anymore. Now, I'm just asking you to get me through this day. Get me through this week. Soon I will graduate. Soon I will go to college. Heal my family, God. Heal me so my kids don't have to grow up like I have. Amen.

Broken Hearts

Loving God, love hurts. Half the time we don't understand what's happening to us. And then when we think we have it figured out—when we've finally found someone who makes us happy inside—it all falls apart. Why did you make love if it's going to hurt like this? Why did you put us on this planet for each other if we have so much trouble getting together? We have a lifetime, God. Give us patience. If we can't find the right person now, give us patience. Help us concentrate on *being* the right person, so maybe we can be found by someone else. Heal this ache, God. It's like a punch in the stomach—it doesn't show, but it still hurts a lot. We are your children. Love us. Amen.

Bullies

God of the underdog, bullies have always been with us. David faced down a bully named Goliath. Herodias demanded the head of a preacher. God, why are there some people who just hate for no reason? What do they get out of putting others down? What is the joy in stepping on someone else? Bullies have been with us since the beginning of time, God, and we can only assume you have a plan. We believe you will take all things, even the actions of hateful people, and make them work to your purposes. In the meantime, God, we could use a little help. Whatever these people need, please give it to them. Show them what they lack so they can stop hurting people. There is no joy in hate. Show them the way, God. We are getting tired of it. Amen.

Burdens

God, we stand at the baggage carousel of life, and sometimes we feel like every bag belongs to us. We have so much to carry. You said we could put our burdens on you, but why would you want this stuff any more than we do? Help us give this weight up, God. Help us trust that you really do know what you're doing. If we could just learn to put some things down and focus on what's important, we would find ourselves moving instead of struggling, being lifted up instead of weighed down. We don't need all this stuff, God. Help us to forgive, to relax, to trust—these will lighten our load. Be there for us, God—we need advice on what to leave behind. We will listen. We will give the heavy stuff to you. Amen.

Busyness

God of rest, when do I get any? I can't do all of this, God. I can't be in two places at once, I don't have three hands, and I can't listen to four people talking to me at the same time. Where are you in all of this? Didn't you hear me? Don't you care? I even dream of being busy when I sleep. I need a Sabbath, Lord. I need a day when my cell phone and my computer and my fax and my laptop are all someplace else. I need just one hour when no one is demanding anything of me. Help me calm this mind of mine, God. Help me learn that always doing more isn't necessarily good for me. Remind me I'm allowed to stop. Amen.

Calling

Father, I believe you have a plan for me. I believe you have a plan for every one of us. But I'd really like to know what you have in mind for me. All I need is a hint—just a little information is all I'm asking. We are all called, God. I know that. You call us, and we get to choose if we stay or go. I'm listening for your voice, God. Really, I am. If you say, "Go there," I will. If you say, "Come here," I will. Sometimes I feel like I'm spinning in circles. I need some direction, a little illumination on the path. Show me what you want, God. I am your servant. Amen.

Celebrations

God of laughter, sometimes it's like we've finally reached the end of a very long tunnel. We were just about to get used to the dark, and suddenly we are out, we are in the open, we have thrown off that claustrophobic feeling that has kept us silent. We are ready to celebrate, God. We are ready to dance. Be the music in our lives, God. Be the strings, the drums, the flashing dance floor. Let us jump and spin and move our feet. We have been waiting for this for a long time. Thank you for bringing us through. Thank you for believing in us. Thank you for lifting us when we've fallen. Now we are going to stand on our own. We are going to party. Amen.

Change

God of choices, we have a tendency to do things the way they've always been done simply because they've always been done that way. But we need change, God. We need something different. If we have to keep moving on like this, we will just dig ourselves into a hole. Show us some light, God—a little flash off to the side so we know you are there and watching. Give us the strength to break away from the comfort of routine and march headlong into something new. Help us take the leap of faith, knowing you will provide a net. Amen.

For Stability

God, what's wrong with routine? We finally get things in order—and something comes along to shake it up. Every day is something different, God. We just need a chance to relax. We need a little consistency. We need a little stability. We need some things that don't explode or break apart when you touch them. If we could get a little routine going, we could get the other parts of our lives together. Then you can change it up all you want. We're out here riding the carousel, when we want to be sitting in a movie theater. Do we have to spin around to change the view? Give us stability when we need it. Amen.

Growing

God, sometimes we go to bed at night, and when we get up, it's like we're different people. Are we supposed to feel this way? Are we supposed to be up one minute and down the next? Ready to scream and laugh and cry and punch someone and hug someone else *all at the same time*? Is that right? This is your plan? We don't get it, God. We've read the books and listened to our embarrassed teachers try to explain the process, but it feels like such a mess when we're in the middle of it. We know we are becoming what we are supposed to be. We know you don't make mistakes, so this must be part of that whole servant-making process. We will take a deep breath. We will calm down. We will trust you know what you're doing. Amen.

Choices

God, you gave us the opportunity to make choices. You gave us brains and hearts and experiences, and we get to use them all to decide things on our own. We are not children, God. We are not holding Daddy's hand. We can decide whether we want to cross the street or stay on the corner. We can decide who we are and what we want to do with our lives. You have given us this ability. We can become whatever we want to be. We don't have to look like everyone else, or talk like everyone else, or be a carbon copy of anyone. We are all original. Thank you for letting us be who we are, God. Amen.

Bad Choices

Loving God, you must have a lot of patience with us. There are people who have decided not to believe in you at all, and you give them that choice. And even we who try to follow you sometimes take a different road. We think we're cruising right along—and then the brakes go out on the truck. It must be hard to watch us make bad choices. You've been around longer than anyone. You have the greatest experience. You know when we make the wrong turn and what's in store for us, yet you let us go. You let us make bad choices. Thank you for that freedom, God. Thank you for letting us learn on our own, however much it may hurt. Amen.

Church

Church Family

God of love, thank you for this family. We don't all have to live under the same roof to be family. We don't even have to share the same blood. This church is family. Family is there when you hurt and when you dance. Family is there when you are lost and when you have found your way home. God, this family is made of love. We don't have to agree all the time. We can argue with love, we can create with love, we can teach with love. That's what family is, God. You have given us one another, and we will cherish one another. We will cherish each moment we have together. We will be your family. Amen.

New Church

God, this building is brick and stone and glass, but your CHURCH is the people who will walk through the doors. We have worked hard to get to this point, God. Thank you for being with us. Let this building be a temple. Let it be a sanctuary in every sense of the word. Let it be a place we use to reach out to the rest of the world, rather than a place where we hide from it. This church building is new, God, but your love is not. Help us show the world your love. Let us use this, your new place, to feed the hungry, shelter the suffering, seek out the lost, and lift those who are down. Thank you for bringing us to this spot, Lord. There is so much we can do from here. Amen.

Coffee

God, right now, let us forget what all the health reports say and simply thank you for the gift of coffee. Thank you for those wonderful beans that are picked, roasted, ground, and brewed to make that wonderful elixir. Thank you for the warmth of the mug in our cold hands. Thank you for the energy and life it puts back in our brains and bodies. Thank you for that warm, wonderful feeling in which every sip seems to flow directly into our blood streams and out to the tips of our fingers and the ends of our toes. Thank you for cream, sugar, and sugar substitutes. Thank you for anything good that goes with coffee. Thank you for coffee ice cream. Thank you for any place that sells coffee. Bless every person who makes or sells coffee. Are you getting the idea, God? Thank you for all your blessings—and at the moment, thank you especially for this one. Amen.

Commitment

Father, it's getting really hard to stay here. It's getting really, really hard not to just walk away. This isn't what we signed up for. This isn't the way it was supposed to be, is it? It was supposed to be fun—this is too much like work. But we will work at this, God. We will recommit ourselves to your purposes. We will hold one another accountable. We will support one another. We will be there for one another, always. Don't leave us now, God. We need you. It's hard, but we will make it work. We will make it work because that is what we are supposed to do. Amen.

Communication

With God

God, we are listening now. We've spent enough time bemoaning our place here. We are ready to shut up and hear what you have to say. We want to talk to you, and we want to listen while you talk to us. We will chat, converse, mind-meld, shoot the breeze—whatever it is, we will be there. We have removed all the things that distract us from your words, and we are ready. Speak, God; your servants are listening. Amen.

With Each Other

God, sometimes it's as if we're yelling at someone who is on the opposite side of the train tracks as the train goes barreling through. We can't hear, and we aren't being heard. We let so much get in the way. We know we have to be ready to listen as well as to speak. If we can't see past our own faces, then we are not doing anyone any good. Help us see what we are doing to build the walls that separate us. Help us stop pointing the finger and blaming others for things we can't hear. Open our minds, our hearts, and our ears, God. Make us your servants. Amen.

Compassion

God of empathy, help us care for one another. This is a cold world some-times, annd there are always so many who are in need. There are those who need food, showers, clothing, and shelter. There are also those who just need a good night's sleep, a kind word, a hug, a phone call, or a moment to themselves. You have shown your love to this hurting world. Help us follow that example. Help us open up instead of closing off. Help us understand we must reach out once in a while, or there may not be anyone to grab our hands when it's our turn down in the hole. Open us, God. Open us—emo-tionally, physically, spiritually, mentally. Guide us to where you need us to be. Help us live out your compassion through our words, our deeds, our lives. Amen.

Competition

God, we can make one another better. As one stone sharpens another, let us help one another become better people. Let us compete and cheer and play and push and endure, but let us do so with respect. Help us value one another's abilities. Move us forward, God. Let us all strive to become the best we can be. If we win, we will celebrate you. If we lose, we will celebrate you. We can learn from our losses as well as our victories, God. As we compete this day, let us do it all in your name. Amen.

Conflicts

Ongoing

God who has joined us together, why can't we see the end of this one? Why does this struggle have to go on and on and on? Just when we think we've finally convinced the other side to see it our way, another roadblock comes up. Are the roadblocks from you? Are we missing something? Help us look past our own limited perspectives. Help us understand the arguments of the other side. Help us remember that just because *we* think something's true, it doesn't necessarily mean you agree. We know our ways are not your ways, that it should be the other way around. Help us learn what you want us to learn out of this, so we can move on. Calm us. Give us peace. Shrillness only hurts the ears and the ego. Let cooler heads prevail. Be among us and let us feel your presence so we can resolve our differences. Amen.

Resolved

That's one down, God. Forgive us when we think of so many new and stu-pid ways to create barriers around and between us. You gave us this planet and these people, but sometimes we mess up. If we spent as much time reaching out as we do holding back, we could feed the world. This conflict is done. We have decided to stop fighting, stop hurting, and stop arguing, and we will focus instead on who made us, who supports us, and who loves us. We will not claim a victory on this one. We will only celebrate that when we decide to resolve the problems that separate us, you win. We are your children, and we will eventually learn to act like it. Amen.

Contentment

God, you have given us what we need. So many of our frustrations come from our unmet desires, not our unmet needs. Jealousy and greed convince us we'll never be happy unless we have what someone else has. You have promised to give us all we need in order to do what we are called to do. Help us learn to be content with what we have. If you give us popcorn, we won't complain there is no butter. If you give us one another, we won't complain someone isn't coming through for us. Stacking up toys and more toys doesn't get us happiness or true friendship or any closer to you. The person who dies with the most toys...still dies. Help us leave behind the selfishness and celebrate the gifts you've handed to us. Amen.

Courage

God, we need you. We need to feel you standing with us. We need your hand on our shoulders. We need to stand up and be counted for what is right. We may get slapped down or pushed to the ground, but if we do, we know you will help us up. You have taught us what is right, God. Give us the courage to make it happen. Give us the strength to stand up for you, whatever it takes. Amen.

Crisis

Personal

God of solid foundations, sometimes it feels like I'm in a hurricane. Everything in my life is chaos. I just want to latch on to something...just one thing that isn't going to get blown around. Just once I'd like to take a step without having the carpet yanked out from under me, God. I'm afraid to move forward, I can't go back, and I certainly can't stay where I am. Does this ever get easier? Am I ever going to have my feet on solid ground again? Your love does not leave me. Thank you for that. No matter how I mess up my life, I know you love me—and if that's all I have, then that's enough. I will start from here. I will stand up and hold your hand, and we will weather this storm together. Amen.

World

God, have you looked down here lately? Can you see us through all the smoke? We are taking your world and tearing it up into little pieces. We are taking the people you gave us to cherish and are killing them. Something is wrong, God. So many lines have been drawn in the sand that the planet looks like a spider web. Somewhere along the line, we forgot how to listen to one another, and we stopped listening to you, God. You may have to talk a little louder over all the noise, but we really need to hear your voice. We really need to feel your presence in the midst of all this. It's dark. There's lots of smoke. Be a light. Be a voice. Help us find our way out of this mess. Amen.

Death

Impending

God, your servant is still here, but we are told it is only a matter of time. And it fills us with questions. We've read the books, we've heard the ideas of those we respect, but still we want to know: Why? Forgive us for our lack of faith, God. We really do believe you know what you're doing. We know that soon you will open your arms, and your servant will soar into them. We will ache down here, God. Help us be here for one another during these difficult days. Give us peace and comfort and love and all we need to accept it and move on. We will be right here, God. We will be right here. Amen.

Occurred

Be prepared, God, __(deceased's name)__ is coming home. Is (her, his) house ready? Do you know what you're in for? Welcome your child, loving God. We have a very distinct hole in our lives, a painful place in our souls that is still tender to the touch. We are grateful that __(deceased's name)__ has no pain, no worries, no sense of loss, no tears, no loneliness—(she, he) knows only the joy of your eternal presence. We experience heart-wrenching loss, but we know all your children must come home. Eventually, all of us will see your face. Eventually, all of us will leave these five senses behind and explode with a thousand new ones. We will miss __(deceased's name)__ terribly, God, but we are happy (she, he) is with you now. Don't wait up. Amen.

Sudden

God, we didn't see this coming. Did you? Did you know this was going to happen? We have faith, God. We have faith that __(deceased's name)__ saw only your face. We believe (she, he) went immediately into your arms. We believe your love surrounded (her, him). Now, surround us with your love. We need help down here, God. It's like having the rug pulled out from underneath our feet. Let us know your peace, God. Let us know your comfort. Help us catch our balance and be there for __(deceased's name)'s family and loved ones. Let us ache, and then let us heal. Let us find a way to make some sense of this. Give us the strength to do what we have to do. Amen.

Tragic

God, we don't get to know everything. We don't understand all the "whys" of this universe. But we believe you know what's going on. We believe you're doing something. Forgive us when we see every horrible thing as a sign you don't care or even don't exist. _____ (event) was a horrible event, God. But we know you were there in that moment. We know you are still there, and you are with us now. We know your (child is, children are) now in your arms and are no longer concerned with the petty distractions of this world. Hold them close, God. Show them to the comfortable chairs and the good food. Let them rest. It won't be long till we are all together. In the meantime, be with us, God. We are left to carry on. It's hard. We need your help. Amen.

Disagreements/Arguments

God, we can't hear each other anymore. We're so intent on saying what we think the other person needs to hear that we haven't stopped long enough to listen to them. We're so hurt by what they say that we never wonder if they have a good reason to say it. Stop us, God. Shut our mouths; open our ears. Let us calm down. Jesus calmed the storms, and the boat got through okay; everyone was safe. We are in a storm now, God—one of our own creation. Please still the winds and steady our boat so we can hear one another and find a solution, not just win the argument. Amen.

Discipline

God, life is hard. Is this what David meant by "thy rod and thy staff"? The rod and staff hurt, God. If you really wanted us to stay on a single road, why did you make so many? Why are there so many exits off the highway? Help us focus, God. We mess up a lot, and it takes a lot to get our eyes back on the road. We believe getting our hands slapped is for our own good. We know you have given us choices—and sometimes we make stupid ones. Help us learn from our failures. We will try again. If it weren't for you, there's no telling how lost we would be by now. Amen.

Discernment

God, it feels like we are constantly coming to forks in the road of life and having to choose. Giving us choices about how to live was your idea, and we are grateful. But remember—it's hard, God. We have experience. We have made good and bad decisions, and we have seen where the road leads. Let us take that experience and make better decisions. We will pray. We will listen. Help us. Amen.

Easter

It all starts here, doesn't it, God? Are you celebrating today? Do you remember what it was like when your Son left the tomb? Did he dance? Did you? No matter what your plan was, it must have been horrible to watch him die. But the resurrection reminds us you are more powerful than death. So we are celebrating, too, God. We are celebrating with sweet candy, and flowers, and music that makes the church windows rattle. Help us celebrate with our hearts. Help us celebrate again tomorrow, and next week, and again some ordinary Tuesday that's still months away. Let us celebrate the resurrection every day. Help us keep it in our hearts, God. Let this be the start of a new life. Amen.

Elderly

God, there is so much wisdom in the eyes of our elders. These servants of yours have been at it for a long, long time. We should look this good someday. Help us hear them, God. They have so much to teach us. They have known you so much longer than we have. They know the stories. They have been through all we have been through and more. They can teach us, advise us, enlighten us. We should be like sponges around them. Help us absorb it all, God. And help us offer our friendship, care, and support when they need it. Thank you for these silver teachers. Help us listen. Amen.

Encouragement

Sometimes it's like we're trying to climb out of a deep hole in the sand. We can see the top from here, but the hole gets deeper when we try to climb out, God. We need your support to see our own way out of this mess we've created. We're not asking to be lifted up and carried into the air. We just need a little rope, God, a little encouragement that we are doing the right thing. Give us a kind word, a little hope, a hint that it's going to be okay—then we can pull ourselves out. That's how it should be anyway. It should be hard. We should have to work at it. We're ready to do that, God. Please just give us a little rope, so we can pull ourselves up. Amen.

Endurance

Just one more step, God. Just one more. God, you are here, and because of that, we know we will get through this. We will stand up and face what's next. Tomorrow is coming, and we will greet that day. We are not down. We are not finished. When it seems like things are piling up in our way, we will go around. We will go through. If we can't go around or through the storm, we will stand here and let the winds blow past us. We will still be here when the storm is over, because you are still here. We wouldn't want you to be alone. Amen.

Enemies

There are people who just love to see us unhappy. Why do they hate us so much, God? What did we do to them? There are people who can't feel important until they put someone else down. Do we do that, God? Have we said things that cause others pain? Forgive us for our behavior, and help us to forgive those whose actions have scarred us. The soul was not meant to carry around hate. Help us put aside the ways we have been harmed. Amen.

Environment

Creating God, you gave us this planet as a playground. Forgive us for what we've done to it. We haven't been responsible stewards of your creation. The planet gives us so much. That was what you intended, but we have to give back, God. We have to give the planet a rest. We have to give the planet a Sabbath. Forgive us for messing it up. Forgive us for turning your sky into mud. This planet will be here long after we are gone. Help us give it reason to be. Amen.

Excellence

God, you put a rainbow of colors in this life—forgive us when we choose beige. You have given us a thousand flavors to live—forgive us when we live vanilla. We can choose to coast through, or we can choose to be excellent. You have given us the choice, and we will make the most of it. You have given us this day, and we will live it fully. You have given us one another, and we will be excellent to one another. Help us see that all things are from you. If we see our lives as gifts from the Creator of the universe, maybe we can learn to celebrate each moment the way we should. Amen.

Excuses

God, you have heard more excuses than there are grains of sand on the beach. We know what you want from us. You gave us your Word. You gave us prophets and preachers. You gave us your Son. And yet still, somehow, we manage to muck it up. Help us take responsibility for our actions and our lives. Help us stop thinking so highly of ourselves that we believe we can do no wrong and everything is someone else's fault. We are not children, God. Forgive us when we act like it. Make us brave. Give us strength to own up to what we've done, to apologize to those we hurt, and to help make the world a better place. Amen.

Extraterrestrials

God, we look out at the sky you created and know the twinkling lights we see are not holes in a black cloth, but actual suns, like the one you gave us.

Is it impossible those suns might warm other faces on other planets? Or are we unique? Are we your sole creations? We will think about such things. We will dream and write books and make movies about such things. We will celebrate your creation, as limitless as it is. Whatever is out there can only come from you. It's all your creation, God. Thank you for the stars in the night sky. Thank you for the imaginations that take us beyond them. Amen.

Faith

God, help us believe in you. Help us have the faith to believe everything you've taught us. You told the disciples they would be safe, but they were still scared of the storm. We hear your words. We say we believe you are in control, but we still struggle with fears and questions. The storms we face are large, but not larger than you. Our problems are many, but not as plentiful as you. You said you would be with us. Forgive our doubts, God. When you tell us we are going to the other side of the lake, help us believe you, no matter what storms come our way. Amen.

God, at some point we will all ask ourselves if this is all just smoke and mirrors. Everyone wonders, sometimes, if you really exist. Is all of this true, or have we been deluding ourselves for centuries? Some say Jesus was no more than a nice man who did nice things. But if Christ was not raised from the dead, then we are all just wandering around in the dark. If all we get out of Jesus is a little warm inspiration, then we aren't worth much. The truth of the matter is you raised your Son. You did it so we would believe. You did it so we could finally understand that everything he tried to tell us was true. The prophets and teachers we ignored were telling the truth, too. Christ was raised from the dead. We believe in the resurrection, and we will change the world. Amen.

Failure

God, we don't always touch what we're reaching for. Sometimes it's like we're standing on seven chairs, stretching up and thinking we are just about to get the tips of our fingers on our goal—and then we bite the dirt. Forgive us for blaming you, God. Forgive us for blaming others. Help us remember you are with us, even in the hard times. Help us learn what you would teach us and start over. Help us find the lesson, gain the knowledge, and dust one another off as we start again. You have said all things are possible through you, God. Help us find what we need to accomplish the task you have given us. Be with us. Encourage us. Support us. We're going to need it. Amen.

Did you see that, God? Did you see the spectacular way we messed that one up? Did you see how we left a giant hole in the wall like some cartoon character? No one is perfect, God. We gave it our best, and we failed. There is no shame in failing—only in not trying again. We can do this, God. We can do it because you are here to help us. We will get our act together. We will make sure your plan becomes reality. What we want is not important. You have a plan, and that's what is important. If we fail, we will ask for your help again. If we succeed, we will give you the credit. Amen.

Family

God of love, putting families together in a small house is like compacting molecules into a small space. We're just going to keep bouncing off one another until one of us explodes. We love these people, God, but sometimes we need a break. Sometimes we need the patience of Job. Have you looked down here? Do you know what we do to one another? These people are our past and our present and our future. We are each other, God—that's what family is. We can build one another up or we can tear one another down. Help us reach out when it's all going bad. We can help one another if we just stop fighting long enough to listen. Help us listen, God.

Fear

God, sometimes fear is healthy. If that big truck coming toward us looks scary, it will make us jump out of the way. But often we seem more afraid of jumping into something new rather than staying where we are. The fear of the unknown seems greater and more paralyzing than the fear of what we already know is going to hurt. So we make ourselves immobile. No going forward. No going back. We just stand in place—till we get hit by the truck. Give us courage, God. You have always been there for us. Peter stepped out of the boat, even though everything inside him knew he would sink. Our fear keeps us from getting closer to you, God. Give us strength. Give us courage. Make us brave. Amen.

Fitting In

God, this world is full of molds, and sometimes it seems like it wants us all to be Jell-O—pour us in so we fill all the cracks and crevices, wait till we're set in place, and then pop us out, so we look like every other Jell-O mold on the table. That's what the world wants, and it's hard not to go along, God. Nobody likes to be the outcast. Nobody likes to stand outside and watch. Help us. Help us understand there is a bigger picture. Help us understand that people who try to mold themselves into someone they are not will be stuck doing that for the rest of their lives. Help us remember that all those Jell-O molds won't be able to stand up to the heat. Give us strength to be whom you have made us to be, God. Whatever we become, we will honor you. Amen.

Following Christ

God, we have made the decision to follow your Son. We want to live with compassion, kindness, gentleness, patience, and self-control. But it's not easy, is it, God? Help us be the ones the world looks to when they want to see you. Remind us being a Christian is not about rules, but about helping, loving, teaching. We will have many opportunities along the way to walk off the path. We will help one another stay the course. We will help each other focus on what's important. We will be servants of the Creator of all things. Amen.

Forgiveness

Of Others

God, we know forgiving is one of your biggies. You want us to forgive others the way we would want them to forgive us. But sometimes that's really hard to do. Sometimes people hurt us by accident; sometimes people just don't think. But God, sometimes people know. They know what they're doing, and they hurt us anyway. It's like that's their goal. They set out to hurt us. We're supposed to forgive that? How does that work? We're going to need you, God. We're going to need strength. We're going to need compassion. We're going to have to get rid of this anger we have inside before we can forgive. Take it from us, God. Take the pain and the anger and throw them away. Help us move forward from this point. We want to be your servants. We will learn to forgive. Amen.

Of Ourselves

God, we've been carrying this around for too long. It's easier to hide than to face ourselves in the mirror, easier to hide than to face you. We can bury the pain down deep inside, but we always know it's there—and now it's getting in the way of everything we do. You know what we did, God. You know everything. You know how much we hurt inside. You know it's making us sick. But we are ready to be done with it. We aren't going to hold on to this anymore. We are ready to get rid of it. We are ready to start fresh and be your servants. What we did was wrong; it feels unforgivable. But we are going to try. And we are going to start with you. We are going to hold out this pain, this guilt, this burning, to you and ask you to take it. We are done. We want to heal. We want to forgive—and to know we are forgiven. We want to move forward. Amen.

Friendship

God, there are people we simply hang out with, and there are other people for whom we'd walk a mile down a blacktop highway in August just to give them a drink of water. True friendship is rare, God. It's a gift from you, and it should be celebrated. We will hold onto our friendships as long as we can, for they are precious, like a rare jewel or a hidden treasure. True friendship will last beyond distance and beyond time. But real friendship must be worked at, tended, and supported. You have given us each other God. We thank you. Now the rest is up to us. Help us make our friendships last, God. We're going to need all the friends we can get. Amen.

Future

All-seeing God, you have this worked out, right? See, it's a little scary down here sometimes. People expect a whole lot of us. They want answers to questions about where we are headed, when we haven't even thought about it yet. They want to know who and when and where and what about the rest of our lives—and we still have 60 more years to go. Do we have to know all this now? Why do people get so intense about this? We need to hear from you on this one, God. We need to know your plan—or at least, we need to know if the plans we're thinking about are possible. Help us find something to say to those who won't stop asking questions. Then help us answer our own questions. Who are we? What are we doing? Where are we going? Can you help us with these, God? Amen.

Gender

God, your creation is difficult to understand sometimes. Life would be so much easier if we could just organize people into file boxes and place them where we want them to be. This whole male/female thing has us crazy, God. You put us on this earth for each other, and day after day it just gets more complicated. Help each of us be brave enough to be who we are, to be what you created us to be. Help us to ignore those who say we "must be this" or "can't be that." We are the handiwork of the Creator of the universe...why isn't that enough for some people, God? We want to be what you have created us to be, but we're going to need help. Amen.

Giving

God, it's not all about us. As much as we like to think the sun rises and sets because we exist...it's not about us. We work for others, not because it makes us feel good about ourselves, but because it's what you said to do. Your hand has blessed us again and again. We have gifts beyond our understanding. We will say thank you for all you have given us by giving these blessings back to you. We will share what we have been given. Amen.

Goals

Striving For

God of endurance, this journey is going to be long and hard. Everything that's worth having is worth working for. We know all things are possible with you. We may encounter every conceivable obstacle on the way. We may face challenges we haven't even thought of and can't prepare for. But we can see our destination, God. Even if it's only in our mind's eye, we can see it. We know what we must do to get there. All we ask now is your continued presence. Let us know you are there. Let us know this is where we belong. Help us along the way because we are going to need it. This is where it starts, God. Bless our journey. Amen.

Achieved

God of endurance, we made it. There were times when we were ready to quit, ready to say, "Forget it," and walk away. We got hurt. We got tired. We got frustrated. But all those things have melted away like a winter's frost in the bright morning sunlight. We've been through the difficult parts; now let us dance. Let us celebrate this accomplishment. Let us give you the thanks, because you were here even when we felt like we were working alone. You picked us up when we fell, gave us energy when we were weary, and turned us around when we got lost. We celebrate your love. Amen.

God's Law

God, we complain too much about the rules. You gave us the sunshine, and we celebrate it. You gave us the rain, and we rejoice in that, too. Even the sky reveals all the gifts you give us. You hand us a world with everything we need to be happy. Then you give us your laws to guide us in that world, and we complain like children. Everything that comes from you is good. With the laws you give us wisdom, as well as the ability to choose our own paths. A lot of times it's hard to see our own failures, God. Keep us safe. Don't let the world around us define what is good and pure and true. We know the things that come from you are what matter most. We will rejoice in your laws, as we rejoice in the rain that ends a drought. We will rejoice in your laws, as we rejoice in the sunrise after a long, dark night. Make our actions acceptable to you, God. Help us show the world the truth about your love. Amen.

Grace

Gracious God, we don't deserve all the good things we get from you. And when it seems like we might get the punishment we really deserve for something we've done, you forgive us. You are the mother who opens her arms after we break her heirloom vase. You are the teacher who gives us one more chance even after we were caught cheating. You are the soda machine that drops us a freebie when we are just pushing the buttons. We don't understand your grace, Father, but we are grateful to receive it. Amen.

Grades

God, the Bible says you don't keep a record of our wrongs—so why does the school? They judge us and categorize us and give us help and deny us funding all based on a bunch of fill-in-the-dot tests. They don't see us, God. You see us. You know us; you don't judge us. Grades are how we get through this life—18 years, then college, then maybe further schooling. It's a long time to go with a letter grade hanging around our necks that everybody sees and uses to make judgments about us. We will study harder, God. We will do what we need to do, because that's the way of this world. We will study, and we will hang our report cards on the refrigerator. And we will be grateful you don't keep a record of our wrongs but rejoice when we do the right thing. Amen.

Graduation

Father, every journey has its milestones—and we have just reached a big one. We can take a breath. We can close our eyes. We can spend a few moments thinking about something—anything—other than school. Thank you for this moment, God. If we look back at who we were on the first day of school, it's a wonder we made it. We remember the bad days. We remember the good days. Tests. Report cards. Good teachers. Bad teachers. Fire drills. Morning announcements. Field trips. It's all part of who we are now, God. All of these experiences have played a role in the kind of adults we are becoming. We are ready to move forward, God. We are looking at the next few years with great anticipation and a little terror. Don't leave us now. We're going to need you. Amen.

Gratitude

God of grace, we don't say thank you enough. We walk though this world and all its beauty, and we don't even notice. We see the bad news on television, and we'd rather complain than ask you for help. You have given us so much. When we stop and consider how this world works, we see the way you have put things together and the ways we have screwed it up. Thank you for your gifts, God. Thank you for the blessings that come every day whether we are aware of them or not. Open our eyes, ears, minds, and hearts, that we may see the gifts you pour out on us in every moment of our lives. Amen.

Guidance

Father, you gave us this world and all its wonders, and we take it for granted. You gave us prophets and teachers, and we chased them away. You gave us your Son with the message of good news, and we refuse to listen. Yet you continue to give to us as your children. Our actions and words show we don't deserve the gifts you give. But like a loving father, you continue to bless us. Help us see all the things you have blessed us with. Help us learn from your Son, who gave his life and asked for nothing in return. Guide us on the path. Bring us closer to you, God. Show us the way. Amen.

God, there is a reason they call us the human race—we are always running. We never stop. We spend day after day trying to move ahead of the next person. We want the fast cars, the expensive toys, the fast lane at the drive-thru. We want to be first. We want to win. But your Son said we need to be last in order to be first. Jesus said we must be servants in order to be the masters. Help us understand this, God. In a world that seems to shine light only on the winners, help us be happy in the shadows. Instead of pushing to the front of the pack, help us encourage those who run beside us. Instead of running around or over those who fall, teach us to stop and help them to their feet. In the long run, God, we need to focus on you and not on what the world expects of us. Give us the strength, the endurance, and the faith to keep running even when it seems hopeless. Amen.

Happiness

God of joy, we are allowed to be happy. We don't have to be dark. We don't have to be angry. We don't have to be sullen. We are allowed to experience the joy you rain down upon this world. Forgive us when we choose to ignore these blessings. You have filled this world with light and laughter and music and joy. Let us absorb that feeling. Let us take it all in and become children of the Author of joy. Let others in this world see us and know you. Amen.

And Knowing It

God, we are happy, and we know it. We are happy, and we are fully aware of that, so we give you the applause. We are happy, and that happiness will show upon our faces. We are happy, God, and we will let the world know by applauding you, stamping our feet on the ground, and shouting praise to you. Amen.

Hard Times

God, we love you and we praise you and we celebrate you. We are in a bad time, God, but we know this doesn't mean you don't love us anymore. Even though our current situation is difficult, we know that doesn't mean you have left us on our own. You are always here. This life you gave us is made up of the good and the bad. We must take both as they come and never fail to give you the thanks. This hard time, this down time, is an opportunity to grow and become stronger. Open our eyes and minds to whatever it is you want us to learn. Show us the light at the end of this darkness; help us begin walking. Walk with us, God. Let us know you are here, even in the hard times. Amen.

Healing

God of love, we need to be made well. There is so much wrong in this world that we are starting to feel it deep inside. We feel it in our hearts. We feel it in our souls. Your Son didn't just heal the bodies of the sick. He healed their souls. We need to feel the healing hands of the Savior, God. We need to feel your love pouring through us and making us whole again. We haven't felt whole in a long time. We take our sickness and our sadness and hold them up for you. Take them from us, God. Take them far away and let us grow from here. Let us feel the beginning of becoming whole. We will become yours. Amen.

Holy Week

God, we don't always look closely at ourselves. We focus on what's down the road or what we left behind us. This Holy Week, help us stop rushing around and look inward. Help us reflect on what kind of person each of us is. Help us understand the choices we've made that have brought us to this point. Help us be quiet and block out the noise and distractions of this crazy world. Come into our hearts. Fill us with the renewal we need to get us through the day. Amen.

Hope

God, sometimes we allow the world to imprison us. We allow others to bury us. We will not stay down, God. We will not stay within these walls of pain. We have hope. You have given us hope. As long as we have hope, nothing can keep us down. Nothing can keep us in the dark. Nothing can take away your love. As long as we have hope, there is no complete darkness, no complete loneliness, no complete sorrow. God of hope, let us know you are here. Amen.

Ice Cream

Creator of all things wonderful, this is one of your better ideas. We know all good things come from you—and this one must have been special delivery. Your love satisfies us like this ice cream, God. On a hot day, your love flows into us and cools and calms the madness that burns inside. We know this is just the smallest taste of what we are in for when we come to your house.

You have tables of this, God. You have flavors Ben & Jerry have never even thought of. Thank you for all the treasures you have put into this life that bring us such joy. You are the God of chocolate, strawberry, and vanilla. You are the God of swirls and sprinkles and cookies and syrup and butterscotch. Thank you for your love, God, that comes in all flavors. Amen.

Idolatry

God, you are important. You are the most important. But we have a tendency to put things ahead of you. We love money, we love stuff, and we seem to pray to anything that will make our piles of stuff bigger. Help us get it straight, God. You build us from the inside out, not the outside in. Teach us to be satisfied with what we have and who we are instead of constantly desiring more and better. We will give glory to you and not to the television billionaire. We will sing our praises to you and not to the one in the spotlight. We will thank you for all you have given us and not the Internet. Help us spend as much time with you as we do with all those things that distract us from you. Amen.

Ignorance

God of common sense, we just don't get it sometimes. You tell us over and over. You show us your love in incredibly obvious ways, yet we still seem to walk around in a fog. Forgive us the stupidity, God. Guide us out of this darkness and into the light of your love that illuminates our minds and the entire world. Help us stop hiding and start believing. Shake the scales from our eyes so we can see what we have been missing. Amen.

Ifs

God of the future, we spend too much time holding back. We live in the past and wonder what would have happened "if"...But we cannot live on ifs, God. There is more to life than wondering whether we made mistakes. We make lots of mistakes. We can't let ifs control us. We must learn to live for the now. You are present *now*. Your love is here *now*. You surround us, love us, lift us, care for us...*now*. There are no ifs with you. We will celebrate you. We will go forward. Show us the way. Amen.

Illumination

God, the Bible says your Word is a lamp unto our feet. We've been stumbling around in the dark recently. Our lives are full of walls to bump into and stuff to trip over. We need illumination. We need to see where we're going. We need the darkness removed from our paths and from our hearts. Make your love-light shine in us, so we are illumined even when we are in the dark. We won't be afraid. You are the God of light, and you will show us the way. Amen.

Image of God

God, we've seen the Sunday school books and the children's Bibles and the movies. We all hold an image of you in our minds whether we talk about it or not. Help us remember we cannot really know what you are. Our senses limit us. Our understanding is incomplete. Someday when we leave this earth and dance with the angels, we will touch your face and see how off base we've been all these years. In the meantime, give us new images of you, and inspire our old ones so we can keep learning, keep growing, keep loving. We are a people that needs to see, touch, taste, smell, and hear. This is how we have to work in order to understand. Forgive us for limiting you, God, but it's all we can do right now. Someday, show us your face. Amen.

Imagination

God, you have given us a mind's eye that can see things not only as they are, but as they could be. You have given us a mind's eye that can see colors on a blank piece of paper. You have given us a mind's eye that can look at a blueprint and see the walls go up. Imagination is a gift from you, God. It is a present. Let us use it to see what we can do with our lives. Let us use it to celebrate one another. Let us use it to see you in all things and all places and all people. You used your imagination to create our world and all that is in it. In the same way, help us to create something good. Let us start with our lives. Amen.

Inner Beauty

God, what we have inside is a reflection of you. These outer shells are barely worth mentioning. The shine rubs off. Teach us to look inside, God. Teach us that deep down in places we don't show each other, you have given us a love that can conquer every trial, a love that can encompass the world, a love that does not dry up. Let us show the world you exist and live deep within our hearts. Amen.

Integrity

God, we get a lot of chances to look out for ourselves by stepping on someone else. There are times when we could help ourselves get ahead, and no one would ever know how we got there. No one would catch us or see what we've done. But you put something deep inside us, God. You gave us an inner voice that tells us when we are doing wrong. You gave us a heart that guides us. Some people can ignore that voice, God. Some people can shut it out and never hear it. We are your children, and we don't play that way. Help us live as you have taught us, even when no one else is looking. Amen.

Job (The Guy in the Bible)

God, what lesson did you want us to learn from your servant Job? Loyalty? Love? Give us the patience Job had, God. We go through hard times, too. We look at this world and see it breaking down, and we wonder where you are. We wonder what the plan is. We know when Job came through his trials to the other side, he was stronger. He was a better servant. He was rewarded. It's tough to be your servant, God. Help us realize our troubles are bearable because you are there to help us. You are there, whether we feel your presence or not. Let us feel your presence, God. We are not Job. We have too little faith. Give us faith and trust, and we will reflect them back to you. Amen.

Job (Employment)

God, thank you for this job. Thank you for the boss who counts the seconds when I'm late. Thank you for co-workers who leave their own work so I have to do it. There are people who don't have a job. But I have this job, God, and good things will come from it. I will learn. I will grow. I will take this experience and make it work out for the better. I will do this job to the best of my ability, even when I don't like it—because that's the quickest way to make a job better, even if it's just a little better. Thank you, God, for this chance to work, to earn money, to gain experience. You have placed this road before me, God. I choose to walk it. Amen.

Joy

God, there is so much in this world to be happy about, yet sometimes all we can see are the things that depress us. Anger is a choice. Sadness is a choice. Help us choose joy. You are the Creator of joy, God. From the moment of creation, you said it was all good. Let us find the good in all things. Let us see the joy in children and follow their example. Let us see the beautiful leaves of the tree and not the dark, hard trunk. Let us hear the music on the radio and not focus on the miles we have left to drive. Turn us around, God. Pick us up and spin us like you did Paul. We are blind, now. Let us see the joy that exists in every living thing. Let us see the joy that surrounds us and follows us and lives in us. Amen.

Judaism

God, we are *all* your children. So much of what we are taught by your Son comes from what he was taught as a boy. Help us remember that you have given us the Old Testament. Help us remember that Jesus was Jewish, and that much of our Christian theology is rooted in Judaism. A son does not ignore his father. Help us hear the Psalms. Help us hear the prophets. Help us hear your wisdom in the Torah. We get arrogant sometimes, God. But there is faith in the traditions. We are not so bold as to presume to know your will. We hope you have an awfully big table, God. Amen.

Justice

God of justice, we need your wisdom. You have given us choices in this world. We can choose our leaders, we can make our laws, we can choose to do right or do wrong. You have left these things up to us. Now we are asking for help. Guide our decisions, God, and help us live with the decisions we've made. Help us remember that our will is not always your will—and let them be as close together as possible. There are so many people ready to tell us what's right and what's wrong. Help us know whom to listen to. Help us have a voice in the crowd. Help us do what is right. Amen.

Kindness

God, when did incivility become socially acceptable? We act as though we have been given a right to be unkind. We can build one another up or we can knock one another down. It's our arrogance that makes us feel like unkindness is merely telling the truth. The truth is that none of us is perfect. The truth is that you have given us one another to cherish or to bash. Help us make the right decisions, God. Let us treat others as we want to be treated. Amen.

{ 114 }

Leaders

God, you have placed certain people in positions of leadership in our churches, our schools, and our nation. The decisions of these leaders affect so many people. Guide their thoughts, God. Guide their decisions. Give them wisdom and compassion and patience and discernment. Help them remember that the choices they make are for all of us, not just themselves. Help us remember we may have to trust decisions we don't understand or agree with. If we don't like the way we are being led, let us do something about it besides complain. Let us offer solutions and not just criticism. Let us offer help and not just hindrance. God, guide our leaders. Amen.

Lent

Father God, help us never forget that Jesus knew his time was coming. The rest of us pass blissfully through life knowing we will die "someday." Jesus knew the time was near, yet he continued to show love and faith. He continually put himself on the line, when most of us would have run away in fear. God, during this time of Lent, give us just one small taste of what it must have been like for him. Help us appreciate the great love your Son had for us—a love that kept him living for others, even when he knew he was going to die. Amen.

Lock-Ins

Father God, we've spent a lot of time in your house, but tonight it all seems so different. It seems like there is always more here than we knew. We can't know all of you, God. There is so much to discover. Yet sometimes we feel like we should know it all. There are those who say they do. They say your name like they are experts, while we sit in the back and feel like we wandered into the wrong class. We can't know all of you, God. Let that be what we love about you. Let us realize it's not necessary for us to understand you fully in order to love you. Amen.

God, your house is so big that sometimes it can make us feel very small. But in the dark, it seems smaller. In the dark, you seem closer. It's like we can reach out and touch your face. Smile, Lord; give us the light from your smile. Let us hear your laughter. Let us know we are heard. We are your servants, God. We are here waiting in the dark for your voice. Let your laughter lead us to you. Let your whisper guide us closer. Light our path, and we will follow your way. Amen.

Loss

God of wholeness, we know loss is part of life. It's part of growing up. But today, it feels like we have a hole deep inside. No one said it would hurt so badly. We don't like feeling empty, God. When does it get better? Does it have to hurt this much to lose (family member, pet, house, friend, etc.) ? There is a space in us, God, that needs to be filled. Send us your love. Send us your light. Send us your comfort so that deep down inside, we will be filled. Amen.

Military Service

God, you have placed in some people a gift of honor and loyalty and a sense of sacrifice many others don't understand. You have given them a willingness to place themselves at risk in order to keep the rest of us safe. Protect your children, God. They are walking into a battle zone. Protect them. Shine a light around them. Wrap your arms around them and tell those who would hurt them, "Not here. Not today." We will do what we are called to do, God. Protect us. Amen.

Prayers

Mistakes

God, sometimes we make little mistakes, like forgetting our homework or dropping a dish. But other times we make big mistakes—the kind where we go running full speed in the wrong direction and leave a giant person-shaped hole in the wall. You are the God of second chances. You are the God who picks us up, helps brush the dirt off our faces, and sets us on the path again. You are the God who will help us clean up the spilled milk. Forgive us when we blame our mistakes on others, God. None of us is perfect. It's a mistake to think we are. Amen.

Money

God, a philosopher once said people only need so much money to live on, and the rest is just for showing off. We don't need to show off, God. But we do need to pay our bills. We can be disciplined, God. We can work within our budgets. We can make ends meet, but we could use a little help. Is it wrong to pray for cold, hard cash, God? Let us feel your presence. What we need most is to know we are not alone and you are in charge. Give us peace, God. Help us trust in you and know everything else will fall into place. Amen.

New Year's Eve

Dear God, it's only a matter of (days, minutes, seconds) now. As we pass into the new year, it feels like another chance. A new beginning. The old year is fading into the past, and we have such hopes for the one to come. God, you must see us this way all the time. We are constantly on the edge of a new life, always counting down the minutes. Give us the chance to make our lives new. Help us put away the things that bring us down and take us away from you. Let us start this new year with a new outlook. Let us know the possibilities. Give us hope. Give us peace. Give us endurance to hold on to the promises and the possibilities. Amen.

Parents

God, there are people in charge of our lives who have watched us since we were born. We have inherited traits from these people, and we don't even know what some of those traits are yet. God, help us remember that our parents were our age once. They felt what we are feeling. They watch us with an experienced eye we don't have. If we were to drive to a new place, we would ask for directions from someone who has been there. Help us treat our parents that way. They understand more than we think they do. Plus, they really do love us. Amen.

Peer Pressure

God, there are so many people who want us to look and act exactly as they do. Help us ignore them, God. They want us to turn away from who we are just so we can be accepted by them, God. But we've checked—and they aren't all that acceptable either. You made us, God. You made us who we are, and we will not become something else just to make somebody like us. If they can't like us for who we are, then we don't really need them. Big words, Father. Now give us the strength to back them up. Give us courage. Give us determination. Give us a sense of the person you created us to be. Make us strong. Amen.

Politics

God, sometimes our nation seems so deeply divided. Politics can be like banging your head against the wall—it just feels good to stop. Help us remember there is no *us* and *them*. We all must live together. We all must exist together. We don't see things the same way, but that's how you made us—and you don't make mistakes. We are different for a reason. Help us come together and celebrate those differences. Help us both lead and follow. Help us make sure the political process works. Guide us so we might become part of the solution instead of just complaining about the problems. Amen.

Priorities

We know what is important, God. Most of our problems come when we put the wrong things at the top of our list—momentary things, things that don't matter in the long run. We have been taught well, God. We are prepared for the next step. Help us not screw it up. We have so much going for us. The future is so bright. We know what's important. Help us live that way. Amen.

Prom

God, there are times in life we will never forget—and this night is one of them. We feel different inside on nights like this. We feel changed. We feel just a little more like the adults we will be one day. This is growing up, God. We grow every day, but tonight it's like we can feel it. Help us enjoy this special time. Let us dance with wild abandon. Let us slow dance. Let us hold hands, smell sweet smells, listen to music, and be in the middle of it all. Let us celebrate being young and alive. We give thanks to you who put us on this earth and gave us this night—and every moment of our lives—as a gift. Stay with us, God. Keep us from doing something stupid. Let us party. Amen.

Purpose of Life

God, sometimes we spend so much time screaming at the rain, hoping you will tell us our purpose, that we can't hear you above our own shouts. We spend so much time asking you to tell us how to live that we forget to just live. Help us be fully alive, God. You have given us so much. You have given us gifts. Help us use them. Help us celebrate them. Help us use what you have given us for your purposes. Then we can find out what our purposes are. Amen.

Racism

Help us accept one another God. Some people hate for no reason. Some people hate for stupid reasons. Help us all see that hatred is based on fear. Help us remember there are no mistakes among your creation. Not one of us is the same as any other. If we hate simply because people are different, then we will hate everyone, and we will be hated by everyone. We were not born for hatred, God. We are yours. We are the ones who say, "Welcome," as your Son did. We are the ones who say, "Let us all be one." There is too much to learn to spend time hating, God. Help us open our minds, open our hearts, and open our arms to the world you have created. Amen.

Rejection

God, when others turn us away, when people we value ignore us, it hurts worse than stubbing your toe on the edge of the bed in the middle of the night. It hurts worse than getting kicked in the stomach. Help us remember that your Son was rejected. Help us remember he was a stone who was thrown on a scrap heap, but now he is the keystone of the world. This pain we feel is temporary, God. This pain will make us stronger. This pain will make us keystones. Use us, God. Let us become the people you want us to be. Make us stronger. We will honor you. Amen.

Resisting

God, there is something pulling at us. You have put us on a path, but there are things off to the side that attract us. Shiny things. Fun things. Things that will be fun momentarily, but won't help us get to where we want to be. Remind us we can rest, God. We can take a moment to rest on this journey, but keep us focused on what's to come. Give us just a hint of what we can be so we can keep following. Keep us moving forward, for we know it can be hard to get back on the path once we've left it. Help us look ahead of ourselves. Keep our eyes on the path. Help us ignore the other voices that call our name. We know who we are, and we know whose we are. Help us act like it, God. Amen.

Respect

God, we will treat others the way we want to be treated. We will treat other people's stuff the way we want our stuff treated. And we will treat you as the Creator of the universe. We will listen to you and follow you. We will respect one another. We will respect ourselves. You have said we are your highest creations, God. Let us treat one another that way. It's so easy to tear one another down. Help us make the effort and lift one another up. Amen.

Road Trip Prayers

For the Start of a Mission Trip

God, bring our minds and hearts into pure focus. We are your servants. Help us remember this above all things. We are your servants. Let us be your hands. Let us be your eyes. Let us be your ears. We are your children. We are here to take care of one another. The world is a scary place sometimes, God. We wonder how it can get so bad. Help us understand that your children must care for one another and, in doing so, bring your presence into the world. Amen.

For the Start of a Fun Trip

God, we stand before you now eager to get on the road. We can't wait, God. We can't wait for the laughter. We can't wait for the fun. Help us take this moment and remember that the laughter and the fun and the friendships and the joy...all of these are gifts from you. Help us show appreciation. Help us remember who to thank. We look to you to get us through the bad times, God. Now help us look to you to be with us as we laugh. Amen.

For When You Pile In

God, we are so full of anticipation that we can hardly stand ourselves. There is enough energy in this circle to power a small city. Help us focus that energy, God. Help us create an atmosphere where we can grow and shine and experience your light. Then, help us reflect that light to others. We are at the beginning, God. All we hope for is ahead of us. Go with us, God. Lift us when we are tired. Guide us when we are lost. Join us when we call on your Spirit. Go with us, God. Amen.

For When You're Broken Down by the Side of the Road

God, we know you don't cause bad things to happen. We know you take all things, both good and bad, and make them work together for the good of those who love you. Give us patience, God. Give us strength. Open our eyes to the big picture, so we see things we would otherwise have missed. Help us see the lessons you would teach us. Let us learn them well, and send us back on our way. Amen.

For When You're Lost

God, we need more than a map right now. In fact, we'd love it if you would send down a flashing neon sign that points us in the right direction. But we are not lost, God. We are in your presence wherever we go. How can we be lost? Calm our anxieties. Place your reassuring hand on our shoulders. Show us the way, but don't let us miss a moment of the experience. Let us take it all in, God. Show us the way. Amen.

For When Everyone Is on Edge

God, there are times when we walk a very fine line. We know that if you compact molecules into a small space, they will eventually explode. Sometimes we feel like we're going to explode. Cut us the slack that we have trouble showing to others. Grant us patience when we are impatient. Help us think before we speak. Let us lift one another up instead of cutting one another down. Let us hold one another close instead of pushing one another away. Grant us space. Grant us respect. Grant us love. We are your children, God. Help us treat one another that way. Amen.

For the Middle of the Trip

God, our trip is half over. We've accomplished a lot, but much is still ahead of us. Let us look at all we've done and smile. Help us focus on what we have yet to do. Give us strength, God. Show us it's not over. Show us we're not done yet. Renew our energy so we can finish the journey we began. Renew our minds so we don't lose focus on what is ahead of us. Amen.

For Patience

The days are long, God. Give us just a little bit of your love, so the next time we think we can't take anymore...we are able to. Give us the ability to deal with those we don't think we can. Give us the courage to get through the situations that seem intolerable. These moments of frustration and aggravation are nothing compared with the good you are doing in us and through us. Open our eyes to the possibilities. Don't let us close our eyes to the world. Don't let us shut down. We are your children, and we need your love right now. Amen.

For Rest

God, the body grows weary. Give us peace. Give us a quiet night. It's hard to keep the soul energetic when the body is so tired. Keep us healthy, God. Calm the thoughts that are running through our brains and give us peace. Relax our tension. Renew us physically, mentally, emotionally, spiritually. Fill us up with your love so we may continue to do all you have asked us to do. Amen.

For Understanding

God, focus our brains in the right directions. Help us open ourselves so we are more concerned about understanding others than about being understood. Give us ears that listen beyond the words. Give us eyes that see beneath the surface. Help us understand one another so we may grow closer. Open the lines of communication so we don't feel like we're talking to a wall. Give us just a small sense of the understanding you give to us, and we will be fine. Amen.

For Guidance

There are a lot of ways to get lost, God. We may be able to point to a map and say exactly where we are, and yet still feel like we're wandering in a dark cave with no flashlight. Call out to us, God. Let us follow your voice. Stand beside us and point. Show us *your* map. Help us go where you would lead us, so we can become what you want us to become. Amen.

For the Last Night

God, we have experienced so much. It's like our brains and souls are on overload. Tomorrow, we will be heading home. We will leave behind all we have done and take with us the memories. We are not the same people who began this trip, God. Help us look forward to the new life that awaits us. Help us reflect the changes in us to those back home. Let the new day be new for the rest of our lives. Amen.

For the Last Day

God, it doesn't seem like we started out just _____ days ago. On the other hand, it seems like we've been at this for a very long time. We are tired and weary, God. But we've accomplished much. We've grown closer to one another, and we've grown closer to your Son. As we leave this place, may we leave behind a small bit of that light that drew us to you. May it brighten the path and lead others to you as well. Amen.

For When You Arrive Home

God, it's over. We're home. Thank you for getting us here safely. Thank you for all we have shared during this time. Thank you for the blessings you have given to us, even if they don't seem like blessings just yet. We are your tired servants, God. Thank you for these wonderful people and the ways you have shown us your presence these past days. Be with us as we step back into our normal routines. Amen.

Safety/Protection

God, it feels like we're on a roller coaster with no lap bar. It feels like we're trying to cross from one cliff to another on one of those rope bridges we see in the movies. We need to feel your presence right now, God. We need to know you are there—watching us, protecting us, guiding us, keeping us from harm. Suddenly, this world feels a little scarier than before, God. Let us know you are still watching over us. We're your children. Let us see you as the playground monitor. Make the bullies go stand by the fence. Blow the whistle. Keep them—and us—from doing stupid things. We need your love around us all. Amen.

Self-Image

Creating God, there is nothing wrong with any of us. Why do we allow others to make us feel like there is? There is *nothing* wrong with us. You don't make mistakes. You don't ever say "oops." You have made us in your image. We are confined by flesh and bone and a measly five senses—yet we are the highest creations of the Creator of the universe. How can we look down on ourselves? How can we fail to see the glory within us? You have made us, God. You don't make mistakes. Help us stop seeing ourselves as anything less than what you created us to be. We will celebrate ourselves, today. We are God's own. You can't beat that. Amen.

Shelter

Loving God, we seek your shelter in our lives. There are all kinds of storms a person can go through, God. Not all of them involve rain and thunder. Some of them involve people and pain. God, we ask that you would be our shelter, because no one else will. Sometimes we feel lost and cold and alone. But in you, we find direction and warmth and belonging. In you, God, we find protection from the people and things that cause us pain. Be our shelter, God. Be our foundation. We will give you the praise. Amen.

Sleep

God, it's okay to close our eyes. Everything that is here today will be there tomorrow. We aren't going to miss anything. You designed these bodies, God. You made us to run and to rest. You made us to get weary and to renew. Give us a peaceful night. Give us good dreams. Give us warm blankets and a soft pillow. Let us experience rest with our whole selves. Wake us in the morning, refreshed. Wake us in the new day as new people. You are the new day, God. Let us wake to greet you and make you part of our lives. Amen.

Spring

God of new life, it feels like we've spent the last few months trapped in a block of ice. It feels like we've spent the last few months in the cold ground, and we're finally digging our way out. The winter was long, God. The light seems new. The warmth feels new. Remind us, God, no one stays down forever. We may feel like we've hit bottom, but we know we will not stay there. Help us adjust our eyes to the light and focus on what comes next. Thank you for this season, God. There is hope in this time of year. There is hope in our lives. Amen.

Stress

God, this is like juggling monkeys. We have way too much to do and way too little time to do it. We demand perfection, and we can't stop and settle for anything less. Help us trust, God. Help us trust others to help share our work. Help us believe in our own abilities to do good work. Calm us and give us a Sabbath when we need it—even if it's only for a short time. Give us a Sabbath day, a Sabbath hour, a Sabbath minute. Help us take just one moment when we think of nothing at all. Help us breathe. Let us feel your touch like a replenishing neck rub. We have so much to do, God. Help us get through. Amen.

Suicide

God of life, it's hard for us to imagine why someone would take him/herself from us. But maybe we have some understanding of it. We have all felt low, God. We have all felt like we're at the bottom of the well. Don't let us lose sight of the hope that is ahead of us. Don't let us forget that every moment is full of possibilities that can take us in a million directions. The future is made of light, God. Don't let us sit in the darkness for too long. Tomorrow will be better. Joy comes in the morning. Help us remember that tomorrow will be better, and the day after that will be a little better still. No one stays down forever, God. We will walk toward our future. Hold our hands so we don't feel alone. Amen.

Summer

God, the warmth of the sun on our skin is a gift. You put this planet in place. You spun it with your finger and set it on a path around a star. Let us feel the warmth of your presence just as we feel the warmth of the sun. Bathe us in your light, just as we are bathed in the light of the sun. Let us stand with our arms outstretched and feel the heat. Let us remember the way we prayed for this last winter. Let the sun make us grow. Let your Son make us grow. We are like flowers, God. Come and walk in this garden. Amen.

Summer Vacation

God, we deserve this. We've worked hard, day after day, for way too long. And this vacation feels like freedom. We understand the hard work is necessary. We understand that if we are going to become better people, better citizens, we have to continue. But this is our Sabbath, God. Help us treat it that way. Help us use this as a time of renewal. Help us use this as a chance to restore our souls, to renovate our lives, to revamp our mindset, so we will be ready when it's time to go back. School is temporary, God. Summers are forever. Let the sun shine on us and make us better servants. Amen.

Sunrise

Creator, your love dawns on us like this new day. Help us see all you have given us. Sometimes we stand in the dark, unaware of our surroundings, until you show them to us. Give us eyes to see the things we miss in our high-speed lives. Illuminate the things we need to see and appreciate, those things we so often take for granted when we stand in the dark. Lord, as this new day appears before us, help us love the gifts we are given—the sights, the sounds, the fragrances. Help us appreciate our family and friends. We know these are all gifts from you, and even though we don't say it enough, Lord, thank you for all you have given us. Amen.

Lord of heaven, we see your sun come up. We know each time the sun rises, it's a new chance for us to live the way you want us to live. We know we have made mistakes, Lord. It's so easy to stray from the path you put us on. Your love is like the day. No matter how many times we wander off in the dark, you take us back again and again, repeating like the sunrise. You have given us another chance. Stay with us, God, throughout this day. Help us love each other as you love us. Take this new day, God, and make us your servants. Teach us. Mold us. Hold us without letting go. Remind us that we walk into this new creation with you at our sides. Amen.

Sunset

God, we stand here amazed by you. When we stop to take it all in, we can't help being amazed. Everything we've seen, everything we've heard—it's all because of you. The winds, the rain, the stars in the night sky, are all your doing. It has been a full day, Lord. We know you take all things both good and bad and make them work for your purposes. As this night begins, let us take stock of our lives. Help us open our minds and hearts to your wisdom. Keep amazing us, God. Amen.

The day is done, God. We've done enough. Center us now. Calm our minds. Help us put all the pettiness aside. The day is done. It is in the past. All the things that bothered us today are no more. If we were hurt, we give our pain to you. If we were wronged, we give our anger to you. If we hurt or wronged someone else, forgive us. We cannot dwell in the past. Jesus is a light to our path, but the path only goes forward. Keep us walking in the right direction, God. Walk with us. Show us the way. Amen.

Talents

God, we have gifts. They are from you. Help us not squander them. Help us understand that the talents we have been given are not a free ride or a backstage pass to a good life. We must practice and use and develop the gifts you have given us as best we can. We will use the talents you have given us and treasure them. We will say thank you by giving some back to you for your purposes. We will take these gifts and use them to show the world you exist. Thank you for your blessings, God. Amen.

Teachers

God, you have looked down from your house and found people who will give their time to make your world a better place, one person at a time. You have found the people who will give of themselves in love until there is nothing left inside to give. You have called them teachers. You have breathed into these people and made them like you. You have made them creative, energetic, and loving. You have given them patience beyond that of ordinary mortals; you have given them eyes that see beneath the surface and ears that hear even what is not being said. Then you made them smart enough to teach your children. These are your angels, God. Help us lift them up and recognize the gift that lives inside each of them. Help us realize that the light that shines in the heart of each one of them is a little piece of you. Amen.

Teamwork

God, if any of us had to do this alone, it would be like trying to clap with one hand tied behind our backs. You have given us a great gift, God. You have given us one another. Together we can accomplish so much more. We can move a mountain if you are with us and we work together. We can get the job done—and laugh while we are doing it. We can sing together. We can reach much further if we are holding hands. We can feed more, lift more, touch more, and clothe more. Thank you for bringing us together. Amen.

Terminal Illness

For the Dying

God, is the room ready? We don't like to watch someone we love go through this. We know this child of yours may be coming home to you soon, and we are trying to prepare ourselves. Don't leave any lag time, God. The moment we lose __(patient's name)__, take (her, him) into your arms. Let (her, him) rocket up from this awful sick place and explode through the ceiling and into your universe. Welcome (her, him) into your loving embrace like a mother hugs her child after coming home on the first day of school. Let (her, him) feel your touch now. Place a hand on (her, his) shoulder so (she, he) knows it's going to be okay. Don't let __(patient's name)__ be scared. Give (her, him) just a little more faith. Then welcome (her, him) home. Amen.

For Ourselves, When a Loved One Is Dying

God, we're not ready to understand this. We are your creations, but we're not you. We don't make the decisions. That's a job we're not qualified for. Forgive our arrogance, God. It's hard to watch someone you love suffer. It's hard to understand why these things happen. We stand in the middle of it all and get angry. We don't know what the meaning of it all is. We need peace of mind, God. We need to feel your arms around us. We need to cry on your shoulder and have you hold us. Tell us everything is going to be okay, God. We need to hear from you. Amen.

Tough Issues

God, we can't ignore the things we need to talk about. We can't bury our feelings. That's like holding a beach ball under the surface of the water. Eventually, we lose our grip and get smacked in the face. Talking about our troubles is uncomfortable and sometimes painful and sometimes embarrassing. Help us get over it, God. We have to make room inside us to grow as human beings, and we can't do that with all the clutter of thoughts and feelings that have no direction. Help us make room, God. Give us courage.

Give us strength. Help us bring things out into the open so we may fill the empty space with knowledge and love. Amen.

Trust

God of love, sometimes we're afraid to trust one another. We have ego issues. We think we have to do everything for ourselves. We've trusted before, and we've been burned, God. We've been hurt, and that makes it hard to trust again. Help us move beyond our fears. Help us forgive. And help us be the ones to move toward trust. Let us show others we can be trusted, and let that become a doorway that allows us to trust them. God, if your children don't learn to trust one another, we will just sit here and stare at one another until we turn to dust and blow away. We cannot move forward—physically, emotionally, spiritually—until we can learn to put aside our pain and guilt and open ourselves enough to trust one another. Amen.

Unconditional Love

Loving God, you don't keep a record of our wrongs. You are patient and kind and don't celebrate when we mess up. You dance when we do things the way we are supposed to. Your Son knew how to love. Your Son loved the people who turned away and left him. He even loved the ones who put him on the cross. We have trouble with that kind of love, God. We put a lot of "ifs" on our love. That's not how you taught us. If you loved us in that way, none of us would ever make it to the kingdom. Thank you for never failing to love us, no matter what we do. We will allow ourselves to be embraced by you, God. We will try to love as Jesus loved. Be patient with us, God. Amen.

Universe

Creating God, we cannot begin to fathom all you have made and how it all works together. We do try, though. We study and think and put our best minds to the challenge, trying to figure out our places in the world, our world's place in the solar system, and our solar system's place in the universe. We have trouble understanding things we can't see, and there is so much more out there than we can see or even imagine, God. And all of it is a gift from you. Help us look to the stars like a child looks at the lights on the Christmas tree. Give us a sense of wonder and awe at your work. Let us imagine and dream about the parts we cannot comprehend, until we have the chance to explore it all together with you. Amen.

Violence

God of peace, your children are hurting each other. We're caught up in a war of words you never gave us. We're caught up in human ideas of you that we are willing to fight and die for. Is that what you wanted? Ever since Cain put Abel down, we have been doing the same. We keep finding new and more frightening ways to hurt and kill each other. We say things we know will hurt. We do horrible things. Maybe we need a spiritual time-out, God. Maybe we need to have our noses put in the corner until we know how to act like children of God. We must be such a disappointment to you sometimes. Give us a sense of peace, God. Give us a sense of belonging so we don't get jealous or envious or angry or frustrated. Teach us to love so we can stop hating. Amen.

Voting

God, what a privilege it is to choose our leaders. We can listen and think and decide who will run things. We cannot take this lightly, God. You have given candidates different gifts and different ideas about how to lead. We get to choose, God. Our destiny is in our hands. We make decisions about who will make the decisions for us. Help us choose wisely. Help us choose with respect for those who will stand at the front and say, "This is what we are going to do." Help us remember that those we disagree with are not our enemies. Thank you for this opportunity, God. Let us use it to make you proud. Amen.

{ 128 }

Waiting

God, we don't wait very well. We are impatient. We don't like to wait for our food at the drive-thru. We don't like to wait for our computers to download files. We want things done in our time. Help us remember that Jesus knew his time was nearly over. While we selfishly demand that things move faster for us, Jesus was praying for time to slow down. All things are done in your time, God. Help us put our lives into the hands of the One who had his hands nailed down. Things will come to us as they come to us. Your will, not ours, God. Amen.

War

God, what is a "just war"? Do you ever want your children to kill one another? War is a kind of chaos, God, in which so much damage is done. It's like when a water balloon hits the sidewalk, and no one can say where all the droplets will fall. But in this case, people are dying, not just getting wet. There is evil in this world, God. Bad people make bad decisions, and the world itself is in danger. People are being killed in great numbers. Sometimes it feels so far away, but other times it feels so close. Is it ever right to kill, God? If we are going to take action, let it be for the right reason. Help us to build up rather than tear down. Help us find better ways to feed and care for one another instead of better ways to kill one another. Be with us and all who are at risk—protect us, give us courage, bless us, and keep us safe. Amen.

Winter

God, this is a season of rest. This is a season of warm blankets and fireplaces and hot chocolate and two hands in one mitten. This is a season for the earth to sleep and plan its coming-out party. The cold is there so we know it's time to go inside. Let us sit closer together. Let us be there to keep each other warm. Let us watch the wonder of your seasons from the window. Let us laugh at the snow; let us feel the cold in our bones and remember that you created all the seasons, not just the ones we like. Let us remember that you have a purpose and a time and a place for all things, just like the seasons. Amen.

Worry

God of stability, we accomplish nothing when we worry. It isn't even a satisfying feeling. We get nothing out of it. Yet, we still do it. Worry fixes problems like a cold soda pop cuts wood. You have things under control. Can we have a little of that confidence? Give us patience because there are things we can't change. But give us courage because there are things we can change. Sitting and wringing our hands just makes our hands hurt. We don't want to hurt, God. Calm our nerves, protect the ones we love, and make us all better servants. Amen.

Scripture Index

This section will be a great help to you in worship—and it may be an invaluable tool for other areas of your ministry, as well. If you want to lead a morning communion service at the winter retreat and the topic for the weekend is God's grace...you can use this index to find verses on grace and then choose the one that will be most effective in your service. You can plug these verses into any service in either of the two volumes of *The Book of Uncommon Prayer*.

Acceptance

Genesis 1:26-28 *I look like God?*

1 Samuel 16:7 *See what's inside.*

Jeremiah 18:6 *Self-acceptance: We're clay in the potter's hand.*

Psalms 8; 56; 139 *God's acceptance*

Matthew 5:43-48 *Love your enemies.*

Luke 2:9-10 *Jesus accepts everyone.*

Luke 6:32-36 *Some are easier to love than others.*

John 4:1-38 *The Samaritan woman*

John 8:1-11 *Throwing the first stone*

John 13:34-35 *Love one another.*

Romans 12:2 *Be yourself.*

Philippians 3:12-14 *Run the race.*

James 2:1-9 *Accept the poor and the rich.*

1 John 4:20 *You can't hate people and love God.*

Affirmation

Psalm 8:3-8 *We are God's.*

Psalm 16 *God will build me a hurricane shelter.*

Proverbs 15:13 *It's all about the attitude.*

Romans 8:17-28 *Be affirmed—God is with you.*

1 Corinthians 13:4-7 *How to affirm others*

2 Thessalonians 1:3 *Paul was always affirming, even when correcting.*

Ephesians 4:7-12 *God has a gift for you—are you ready?*

Angels

As Helpful Spirits

1 Kings 19:5

Luke 16:22

Acts 12:7-11; 27:23-24

Hebrews 1:7-14

As God's Messengers

Daniel 8:16-12:13

Matthew 2:13, 20

Luke 1:19, 28

Acts 5:19-20; 8:26; 10:5; 27:23

Jesus and Angels

Matthew 1:20-21; 28:5-7

Luke 1:30-31; 2:10-12; 24:23

Acts 1:10-11

Anger

Genesis 4:3-8 *Anger affects our behavior.*

Ephesians 4:26 *Don't hold on to it.*

James 1:19-20 *Anger doesn't bring the life we should live.*

Arguments

Proverbs 15:1 *Do your words make it worse?*

Galatians 5:22-23 *How to stop an argument*

James 4:1-6 *Daddy, where do arguments come from?*

Attitude

Psalm 98 *God does not make mistakes. Everything is good.*

Luke 14:15-24 *Attitude determines your seat at the table.*

Philippians 2:14-15 *Do everything without complaining.*

Authority

Deuteronomy 11:18-21 *Listen—this stuff is important.*

Psalm 50 *Who's the boss?*

Proverbs 23:13-14 *Nothing wrong with a swat on the bum*

Colossians 3:23 *Ultimately, God is in charge. Not you.*

Behavior

Matthew 7:3-5 *People who live in glass houses shouldn't throw stones.*

Matthew 20:1-16 *You don't get to decide "when."*

James 1:19 *Quick to listen, slow to speak*

Belief

Genesis 15:6 *Belief = righteousness.*

Matthew 7:21 *Actions and belief go together.*

John 3:16 *This is the biggie.*

John 20:31 *Why believe in Christ?*

Romans 14:1-23 *Belief varies from person to person.*

Bible

Romans 1:16 *The Bible has power.*

2 Timothy 3:16 *It's all inspired by God.*

Hebrews 4:12 *Scripture is a sword.*

James 1:22 *Don't just listen to the words—do them.*

2 Peter 1:20 *We're not making this stuff up.*

Bullies

Deuteronomy 9:2-3 *You can stand up to bullies.*

Proverbs 3:29-33 *Twisted souls.*

Psalm 136 *Persistence pays.*

Ecclesiastes 10:10 *Nerds win!*

Ephesians 5:11 *Don't keep it inside. Tell someone.*

Change

Malachi 3:6 *God doesn't.*

2 Corinthians 1:3-4 *When the sands shift, seek God's help.*

Philippians 4:11-13 *God helps us be content.*

Clay

Isaiah 64:8 *We are clay in God's hands.*

Jeremiah 18:3-6 *When we are broken, God can remold us.*

Romans 9:20-21 *Does the clay question the potter?*

Cliques

Philippians 2:3-6 *Gather together for the right reason.*

Romans 15:7 *Jesus excluded no one.*

Galatians 3:28 *We all belong to God.*

Commitment

Psalm 37:4-5 *God wants our complete devotion.*

Mathew 16:26 *Don't be a sell-out.*

Mark 9:33-35 *You don't have to be first all the time.*

Mark 10:31 *Does it bother you that God starts from the back of the line?*

Compassion

Luke 10:25-37 *The Good Samaritan*

1 Corinthians 13:4-5 *R-E-S-P-E-C-T*

Titus 3:8 *Sometimes you have to do what's right, even if it's not fun.*

Confidence

Psalm 46:1-3 *God will give it to you.*

Conflict

1 Kings 3:16-28 *A wise judge settles a conflict.*

Psalm 106 *God settles things.*

Proverbs 12:20 *God likes the peacemakers.*

Proverbs 15:1 *Speak softly.*

Matthew 5:9 *Peacemakers = God's children.*

Romans 12:4-5 *We must learn to work together.*

Cooperation

Mark 10:31 *The last guy across the finish line is the winner.*

1 Corinthians 12:12-27 *If we're going to do this, we have to work together.*

Colossians 3:7-11 *You KNOW how to live right. Do it.*

Galatians 6:2-6 *Guess who's responsible for who you are? YOU!*

Ephesians 5:21 *It's all about give and take. Do both.*

Hebrews 12:14-16 *Look out for each other.*

Conversations

Psalm 15 *Always tell the truth.*

Proverbs 2:3-6 *Seek wisdom, and you will find it.*

Proverbs 13:3 *Be careful with your words.*

Colossians 4:5-6 *Words full of grace*

1 Timothy 4:12 *Teenagers can lead!*

2 Timothy 2:7 *Stay with the program. God will show you the answer.*

Titus 2:7-8 *Choose your words carefully.*

James 1:19 *Quick to listen, slow to speak*

James 3:9-12 *Garbage in, garbage out*

Dating

Proverbs 4:23 *Look after your heart. Be careful whom you give it to.*

Romans 7:24-8:26 *Controlling yourself is not easy.*

1 Corinthians 13:4-7 *A guide for dating*

1 Timothy 4:12 *Be an example to others.*

2 Timothy 1:7 *If you've got it, flaunt it.*

Titus 2:6-8 *Lead by example.*

Dealing with Idiots

Psalm 73 *Listen to God, not stupid people.*

Proverbs 9:6 *Don't be one.*

Proverbs 14:7 *Stay away from them.*

Death

Psalm 23 *God is always with you.*

Psalm 42:1-11 *When someone you love dies*

Matthew 6:33-34 *Live for today.*

Matthew 25:46 *Death is not the end.*

John 3:16 *Believe and you will never die.*

Philippians 1:20-26 *To die is to win.*

James 4:14 *Life is short.*

Decisions

Genesis 2:15-17 *God gave us the choice.*

Proverbs 18:15 *Seek wisdom before deciding.*

Proverbs 18:17 *First choice is not always the best choice.*

Matthew 6:24 *You get to choose your own path.*

Matthew 9:9 *The hardest ones seem easy.*

Matthew 27:24 *Own up to yours.*

Romans 12:2 *Don't conform to the world's view.*

Romans 13:1-6 *There are certain responsibilities that go along with growing up.*

1 Corinthians 6:12 *Take charge of your own life.*

1 Corinthians 8:9 *Others are watching you.*

James 1:5 *Ask God.*

Colossians 3:23-24 *Do it in the name of God.*

Depression

Psalm 27:13-14 *You won't be depressed forever.*

Psalm 73 *God will pull you out of it.*

John 16:33 *Everybody gets depressed.*

Philippians 4:4-9 *Snapping out of it*

Disabilities

1 Samuel 16:7 *See beyond the physical.*

Psalm 139:13-16 *We are all created beautiful.*

2 Corinthians 11:24-28 *We can overcome.*

2 Corinthians 12:7 *Thorn in the flesh*

Philippians 4:12-13 *Quit your griping.*

Hebrews 12:12-13 *Help one another.*

1 John 3:2 *We will all be like Jesus someday.*

1 John 3:16 *Take care of one another.*

Discouragement

1 Samuel 1:10 *Take it to God.*

1 Samuel 1:18 *God will take it from you.*

Romans 8:28 *God will make it turn out right.*

Philippians 1:12-14 *There may be a reason.*

2 Timothy 2:1-7 *Don't take it too hard.*

Hebrews 12:1-3 *Remember Jesus when you're discouraged.*

Divorce

Matthew 19:4-6 *Man and woman belong together.*

1 Corinthians 13:4-7 *Is there love?*

Drugs

1 Corinthians 6:19-20 *Your body is a temple.*

Galatians 5:1-26 *You can choose your own path. Don't be stupid.*

James 4:14 *Life is short enough.*

Ego

Isaiah 33:15-16 *Attitude is everything.*

Jeremiah 9:23 *Even if you are that cool, you don't have to talk about it all the time.*

Psalm 145 *Take time to thank God.*

Romans 2:1 *How's that whole judgmental thing working out for you?*

Romans 12:1-3 *Be yourself, not perfect.*

1 Corinthians 5:6 *Arrogance multiplies.*

Encouragement

Proverbs 12:25 *Use kind words.*

Romans 8:28 *God will use all things for good.*

Romans 8:38-39 *Nothing can separate us from God.*

1 Thessalonians 5:9-23 *A guide for encouragement*

Hebrews 12:1 *Lose the baggage.*

Employment/Career

Psalm 69 *I'm in over my head here, God. Help!*

Proverbs 4 *Advice from Dad*

1 Corinthians 12:4-7 *Everybody gets gifts. Use them.*

Failure

1 Samuel 16:7 *God sees our hearts.*

Psalm 42:5-6 *Turn to God when you've failed.*

Proverbs 28:26 *Lack of wisdom leads to failure.*

Isaiah 31:1 *Trust God or you will.*

Haggai 1:5-6 *Some people see it everywhere.*

Faith

Psalm 8 *Everything is because of God.*

Jeremiah 29:11 *Don't worry. God will look after you.*

Matthew 17:20 *Just a little bit can move mountains.*

1 Corinthians 16:13 *Stand firm.*

James 1:3 *You are stronger when it gets tested.*

Family

Psalm 133 *Life is good when families get along.*

Proverbs 11:29 *Don't mess with the family.*

Matthew 12:46-50 *Your spiritual family*

2 Corinthians 6:11-13 *Open up a little and see what you can learn.*

Ephesians 6:1-4 *Families! Shut up and listen!*

Fear

Psalm 23 *Comfort in times of fear*

Proverbs 29:25 *Who cares what others think?*

Mark 4:35-41 *Jesus calms the storm.*

2 Corinthians 7:5-6 *God offers comfort in distress, often through each other.*

Feeding the Hungry

Matthew 14:19-21 *Jesus feeds the five thousand.*

Matthew 25:31-45 *As you've done to others, you've done to me.*

James 2:14-18 *Faith and deeds together*

Forgiveness

Psalm 32 *Forgive yourself—no guilt trips.*

Psalm 51 *God's forgiveness is complete.*

Jeremiah 31:33-34 *God's promise to forgive*

Matthew 18:21-35 *Forgive always.*

Luke 11:2-4 *The Lord's Prayer*

Luke 23:34 *Jesus forgives his enemies.*

1 John 1:9 *Confess and be forgiven.*

James 2:13 *We get what we give.*

Friendship

Job 2:11-13 *Sometimes you don't even have to say a word.*

Proverbs 17:17 *Friends always love.*

Proverbs 18:24 *Find one true friend.*

Proverbs 22:24 *Anger loses friends.*

Proverbs 27:6 *Be honest with friends.*

Proverbs 27:9-10 *Friends care for one another.*

Proverbs 27:17 *Friends build up one another.*

Mark 2:3-12 *Four good friends*

John 15:13-15 *Great friends (It doesn't necessarily mean death.)*

Acts 20:35 *Think about this: You actually get more by giving.*

1 Corinthians 13:4-7 *A guide for friendship*

James 2:8-9 *Love others as you love yourself.*

Galatians 3:28 *Our differences will pull us apart if we let them.*

Galatians 6:2 *Help one another out.*

Hebrews 10:24 *Sometimes you have to work at it.*

Future

Genesis 12:1-4 *Our future is so bright.*

Deuteronomy 31:1-6 *Why worry? God is here forever.*

Psalm 105 *God has it covered.*

Jeremiah 29:11 *God has a plan.*

Matthew 6:33-34 *Forget about it. Focus on God.*

1 Corinthians 2:9 *Only God knows.*

Hebrews 13:5-8 *Christ is always, always—always—here.*

Gifts

Psalm 68 *God gives glory and power.*

Ecclesiastes 2:26 *The gift of wisdom*

Isaiah 42:5-6 *The universe—God's gift*

Ezekiel 11:19 *God gives a new heart.*

Daniel 2:21-23 *Need it? Ask for it.*

Matthew 11:28 *God gives you energy.*

Matthew 25:14-29 *What will you do with your gifts?*

John 16:23-24 *God gives what we need.*

Romans 11:29 *God's gifts don't wear out.*

Romans 12:6-8 *Be what God made you to be.*

1 Corinthians 1:5-7 *God's gifts are all around you.*

1 Corinthians 12:4-11 *Every person gets a special gift.*

1 Timothy 6:17 *God's gifts are better than what you get here.*

James 1:1-18 *Your problems and trials are gifts.*

1 Peter 4:10 *Share with others what God gave you.*

2 Peter 1:3 *Just knowing God is a gift.*

God's Nature

Psalm 53 *Preach there is no God, and God will preach there is no you.*

Isaiah 44:6-20 *God is God. There is only one. How much more do you need?*

Romans 11:34-36 *You don't have to understand God to love God.*

Grace

Psalm 89 *God takes care of his own.*

2 Corinthians 5:16-21 *Look inside a person. Give 'em a new chance.*

Romans 4:4-5 *Too big to lift? Ask God. He's pretty strong.*

Matthew 20:1-16 *We don't deserve it, but we get it anyway.*

Romans 3:22-24 *Nobody's perfect.*

Romans 5:20 *The more we mess up, the more grace we get.*

Ephesians 2:8-9 *You can't earn it.*

Grades

Exodus 31:2-11 *Some of God's gifts are for you alone.*

1 Samuel 16:7 *How God sees us is different than how the world sees us.*

Romans 12:2 *If everybody else jumped off a bridge...*

Growing Up

Psalm 139 *We are all the unique creations of the Creator God.*

Proverbs 19:21 *Make plans, but God's come first.*

Proverbs 21:5-6 *Good things may take time.*

Jeremiah 29:13 *If you are willing to work for it, you'll get it.*

Luke 15:11-32 *Avoid impulsive behavior.*

1 Corinthians 13:11 *Put away childish behavior.*

2 Corinthians 1:3-4 *God is there in hard times, too.*

Galatians 5:13-15 *Independence costs.*

Ephesians 4:2 *You'll get there soon enough.*

Philippians 2:13 *God will give you the strength to do what is right.*

1 Thessalonians 5:13-15 *Respect*

1 Timothy 4:12 *Don't let anyone look down on you.*

James 4:14 *Tomorrow never knows.*

Heaven

Genesis 1:1 *Guess who created it?*

Matthew 13:47-49 *Who gets in?*

Heroes

Ezekiel 22:30 *I need a hero!*

Isaiah 5:20-22 *Bad guys lose. Always.*

Mark 8:35 *Put others first.*

Hope

Psalm 3:2-6 *God gives us hope.*

Romans 8:17-39 *Paul explains hope.*

Romans 12:12 *Be joyful in hope.*

1 Corinthians 13:13 *One of the big three*

1 Corinthians 15:54-56 *The answer to death*

2 Corinthians 4:18 *Think of what is unseen, not what is seen.*

Ephesians 4:4 *One spirit, one body, one hope*

1 Peter 3:15 *One of the keys to meeting Jesus*

1 John 3:2 *We shall be like Jesus.*

Integrity

Genesis 43:1-15 *Joseph's father shows it.*

Leviticus 19:11 *Rules for life*

Psalm 24:1-6 *You need it to stand before God.*

Job 2:9-10 *Everything—good and bad—comes from God. It's ALL a gift.*

Job 22:23-29 *Don't let the world get you down.*

Proverbs 10 *You want to be happy? This chapter is "Plan A."*

Proverbs 19:1 *Integrity is greater than wealth.*

Daniel 3:1-30 *God can help you keep it.*

Matthew 6:5-6 *It's prayer, not a Broadway production.*

Luke 8:4-8 *Good roots = good crops.*

Luke 16:10-11 *Faithful in the little things, faithful in the big things*

Acts 5:1-11 *The consequences of having none*

Philippians 4:8 *Be true, noble, and honest—and you will be whole.*

1 John 5:14-15 *Be honest before God, and you'll get what you need.*

Joy

Ecclesiastes 2:26 *A gift from God*

Matthew 7:1-6 *It's called the boomerang effect.*

Luke 18:16 *We must learn to be like children.*

2 Corinthians 5:16-21 *A note from the God of second chances*

Ephesians 2:11-22 *You're a servant—act like it.*

Ephesians 6:11-13 *Our struggle isn't against each other.*

{ 140 } ## Justice

Deuteronomy 33:20-21 *God will bless those who are obedient.*

Job 34:11 *We get what we deserve.*

Psalm 37 *To God, the bad guys are a joke.*

Psalm 106 *God will "take care" of those who oppose him.*

Proverbs 1:24-30 *There is a time for punishment.*

Jeremiah 17:10 *God sees a person's heart.*

John 6:37-38 *God's purpose, not ours*

1 Peter 2:17 *It's all about respect.*

Living

Psalm 27 *Celebrate being alive.*

Isaiah 33:15-16 *Live right. Get cookies.*

1 John 4:7-12 *Love = God. It's not hard math.*

Love

Matthew 5:3-10 *The kid whose lunch money gets stolen is going to get the really, really GOOD cookies.*

Luke 19:10 *The lost will be found.*

John 3:16 *This is what it's all about.*

Romans 8:35-39 *Nothing can separate us from God's love.*

1 John 4:8 *God is love.*

Loving God

Exodus 20:5-6

Deuteronomy 6:5

Joshua 23:11

Psalm 18; 31; 63; 73; 91; 97; 116; 145

Proverbs 8:17

Matthew 22:37-38

Mark 12:29-33

Romans 8:28

Philippians 1:9

2 Timothy 1:7

1 John 3:17-18; 4:16-5:3

Loving Jesus

Matthew 10:37-38; 25:34-40; 27:55-61

Mark 9:41

Luke 7:47

John 14:21-23; 15:9; 16:27; 17:26; 21:17

Ephesians 3:17-19; 6:24

Philippians 1:9

Loving One Another

Leviticus 19:18

Psalm 133

Proverbs 10:12; 15:17; 17:9

Song of Songs 8:6-7

Matthew 5:41-47; 19:19; 25:34-40

Mark 12:30-33

Luke 6:31-35

John 13:34-35; 15:12-13, 17

Romans 13:8-10

1 Corinthians 13:1-14:1; 16:14

2 Corinthians 8:7-8

Colossians 3:12-14

1 Thessalonians 3:12

1 Timothy 4:12

1 Peter 4:8

1 John 2:9-11; 3:11; 4:12

Maturity

Jeremiah 18:6-11 *God is the potter; we are the clay.*

Mark 4:26-28 *Seeds grow. What are you planting?*

Romans 12:3 *God blesses us. We say thank you by how we live.*

Romans 14:12 *Rake your own yard before you complain about your neighbor's.*

Ephesians 4:11-16 *Growing up is part of the whole "servant" thing.*

Philippians 1:27 *How do you act when the teacher leaves the room?*

Colossians 3:23 *Do everything as if you were doing it for God.*

Mistakes

Genesis 4:6-9 *Don't lie about them.*

Proverbs 28:13 *Admit and learn.*

Missions

Genesis 47:13-25 *Joseph feeds the hungry.*

1 Chronicles 16:23-24 *Proclaim God to the world.*

Jonah 1:1-3:9 *The story of Jonah*

Psalm 96 *A song for missionaries*

Matthew 5:13-16 *Let your light shine.*

Matthew 14:19-21 *Jesus feeds the five thousand.*

Matthew 24:14 *Take the gospel to the world.*

Matthew 25:34-40 *Sheep and goats*

Matthew 28:19-20 *The "Great Commissioning"*

Acts 6:2-4 *Feeding the hungry*

Acts 26:14-18 *Saul becomes a missionary.*

1 Corinthians 13:1 *Without love, the rest doesn't matter.*

Philippians 2:4-11 *Look out for each other.*

James 2:14-19 *Real faith is more than just talk.*

1 John 3:16-18 *Back up words with actions.*

Parents

Deuteronomy 5:16 *Learn from the Commandments.*

Proverbs 11:14 *Get good advice.*

Luke 14:16-19 *"I have responsibilities" usually means you're avoiding responsibility.*

Luke 16:10-12 *Earning parental trust*

1 Corinthians 13:11 *Everybody grows up.*

Ephesians 6:4 *Take it easy on your children.*

Colossians 3:20 *Yes, you have to listen to them.*

Hebrews 5:14 *You don't get to grow up all at once. Take your time.*

Hebrews 12:15 *Parenting: the job that never ends*

1 John 3:18 *Show them you love them.*

Peace

Leviticus 9:18 *Working for peace isn't always pretty.*

Psalm 120 *A man of peace*

Psalm 147 *God created it.*

Isaiah 2:4 *War is over.*

Matthew 5:9 *Blessed peacemakers*

Matthew 5:25 *Settle arguments yourself.*

Matthew 5:38-41 *Love your enemies.*

Luke 2:14 *The angels announced it.*

Luke 6:31 *The golden rule: a recipe for peace.*

Romans 12:18 *It's our job.*

James 3:17-18 *Peace brings righteousness.*

Peer Pressure

Genesis 39:1-9 *Don't be pressured.*

Psalm 139 *We are unique and loved.*

Matthew 6:33-34 *Resisting peer pressure*

Romans 12:1-2 *Live every part of your life like a child of God.*

Romans 12:3-21 *We all have a place.*

1 Corinthians 6:19-20 *The body is a temple.*

1 Corinthians 15:33 *Be careful whom you hang out with.*

Philippians 4:4-7 *Pray for strength.*

James 1:2-4 *Trials bring strength.*

Politics

Daniel 4:31 *Kingdoms fall. Governments change.*

Romans 13:1-2 *Authority deserves respect.*

1 Peter 3:15-16 *If you don't do anything to get on the cover of a tabloid, you won't get on the cover of a tabloid.*

Prayer

Psalm 55:1 *God will listen.*

Matthew 5:44 *Got enemies? Pray for them!*

Matthew 6:5-6 *It's not for show.*

Luke 11:1-4 *The Lord's Prayer*

Luke 22:40 *Ask God to free you from temptation.*

Colossians 4:2 *Be devoted to prayer.*

1 Thessalonians 5:17 *Don't ever quit.*

James 5:16 *Pray for one another—it works!*

Relationships

Psalm 34 *God is like heart glue.*

Proverbs 17:12-14 *Be careful of the company you keep.*

Philippians 2:12-13 *Sometimes getting along takes a little effort on your part.*

Philippians 4:12-13 *Appreciating what you have*

Ephesians 4:25-5:10 *No more lies*

James 2:12-13 *Live a good life, and you'll live a good life. (Yeah, it's that simple.)*

Responsibility

1 Corinthians 9:24-27 *Persistence pays off in the long run.*

Galatians 6:7-10 *You get what you plant, so don't put off the planting season.*

Colossians 4:2 *Pay attention!*

Revenge

Job 18:5-21 *The bad guys lose in the end. Always.*

Romans 12:19 *Payback is for God, not you.*

Self-Esteem

Genesis 1:26-27 *You look a lot like your Father.*

1 Samuel 16:7 *God has different standards than we do.*

Psalm 139:13-16 *You are an amazing creation.*

Sex

Genesis 2:22-24 *God made us as sexual beings.*

1 Corinthians 6:12 *Draw your own lines.*

1 Corinthians 10:12-13 *Temptation is normal.*

1 Thessalonians 4:3-7 *Behave yourself.*

Soul/Spirit

Job 32:8 *The breath of God*

Proverbs 20:27 *Show our true selves to God.*

Ecclesiastes 1:8 *Even our souls can get tired.*

Ecclesiastes 12:7 *The body dies; the soul goes back to God.*

Isaiah 26:9 *Needing God's help*

Matthew 10:28 *You can kill the body but not the soul.*

Matthew 26:41 *The spirit is willing...*

Luke 23:46 *The last words of Jesus*

Romans 7:14-25 *My spirit says "yes"; my body says "no."*

1 Corinthians 2:11 *Know God by his Spirit.*

2 Corinthians 4:6-7 *We're like treasure in jars of clay.*

Spiritual Gifts

1 Corinthians 12:1-31 *What are they, and how do I use them?*

Galatians 5:22-23 *Fruits of the Spirit—you need them all.*

1 Timothy 4:14-15 *Gifts: Use 'em or lose 'em.*

Success

Proverbs 3:5-6 *How to find it*

Ecclesiastes 2:4-11 *Chasing the wind*

Romans 12:2 *Be your own person.*

Philippians 3:13-14 *Don't ever stop trying.*

Colossians 3:17 *Do everything in God's name.*

Temptation

Psalm 119 *God helps make us who we are.*

Matthew 4:1-11 *Jesus faces temptation.*

James 1:2-18 *Whatever doesn't kill you only makes you stronger.*

Thankfulness

Jonah 2:9 *Give thanks, even from the belly of the whale.*

Psalm 92:1-5 *Thank God for his gifts.*

Luke 17:11-19 *The healed leper thanks Jesus.*

1 Thessalonians 5:18 *Give thanks for everything.*

Trust

1 Samuel 17:34-37 *God will deliver.*

Romans 8:28-39 *Trust God to know what he's doing.*

Worry

Ecclesiastes 4:4-6 *Worrying solves nothing.*

Matthew 6:25 *Don't worry about what you wear.*

Matthew 6:34 *Tomorrow will take care of itself.*

Luke 12:24-34 *Consider the birds.*

Philippians 4:6-7 *Pray about your worries.*

Wisdom

Jeremiah 17:10 *God knows what you really need.*

Matthew 6:33 *Shortcuts will often lead you into a brick wall.*

Luke 12:15 *Better clothes don't make you a better person.*

See also: Proverbs 1:5, 7, 20-33; 2:1-20; 3:13-26, 34-35; 4:4-13; 7:2-4; 8:1-9:6, 9-12; 10:8, 13-14, 21, 23; 11:9, 12; 12:1,8, 15; 13:14-16; 14:6-8, 16, 18, 33; 15:2, 7, 14, 33; 16:16, 20-24; 17:10, 24; 18:15; 19:8, 20; 21:11; 22:17-21; 23:12, 19, 23; 24:13-14; 28:5, 7; 29:3.

Private Prayers for Youth Workers

Yes, you *do* need your own set of prayers. Why? Because no sane person would ever choose to do this sort of work of their own accord. You heard *the call*, and you answered. God put you in this place, but he didn't promise it would all be fun and games. You need to maintain your own prayer life if you're going to have anything to offer to the kids you're with.

These prayers are for you. Use them as a kick start, a way to get the words moving. Think of them as a launching pad for your own time with God. Pray them over and over, take comfort in their meaning, and find solace in their words.

Find that private place—whether it's in your home, your church, or your office. Take this book with you up into the bell tower or down by the ocean. If you like to have some sort of meditative music playing during your "God-time," you'll find several tracks on the CD with this book will work well. Try "Seeds of Hope," "The Lord's My Shepherd," "When I Survey the Wondrous Cross," or the instrumental "Stars." You can also find some nice meditative music on the CDs titled *Benediction* and *Vespers* by Jeff Johnson. You might also try tracks from *A Collision* by David Crowder Band or *Just George* by Lost and Found.

A Prayer before the Board Meeting

God, you put the universe together.

You understood that the tree must grow near the water.

You put the desert far enough away from the ocean.

You hung the stars like some gigantic mobile, and then blew your breath across it so it all started to spin.

But, God, you didn't have to do any of this with a church committee.

I'm trying, God. I really am.

I can't stay awake in these meetings most of the time, and when I do stay awake, it's only because I'm getting yelled at.

Some of these people come to this meeting with lists, God.

Some come with nothing to do except prattle on and on.

I don't administrate well, God.

Help me.

(*Lift up some specific things you are going to have to address in this meeting.*)

Meetings like this are what make my job a "job," God.

Make me strong.

Give me patience.

Above all else, Father, give me understanding. If I can understand where these people are coming from, maybe I can help them understand me and what I do.

If I understand them better, maybe I can help them get what they need.

Help me focus on others, God, and not so much on myself.

This is just one meeting. I can get through this. Then I can go back and work with your children.

Amen.

A Prayer after the Board Meeting

God, does anyone but you understand?

Why do I always have to explain myself?

Why do I always lose focus?

Why do these people think I am not a "real" servant, and my youth are not "real" members of your holy church?

These meetings suck the life out of me, God.

Fill me.

Rejuvenate me.

Lift my spirit out of the well.

(Take a moment and give God the concerns that came out of the meeting. Don't hold back. Be angry if you want. Let God know your fears, hopes, and dreams for this youth group.)

The meeting is over, God. Thank you.

They didn't fire me. Thank you.

I still want to be your servant. Thank you.

Now I have this new list of things they want me to do.

I can do this.

You'll help me, won't you, God?

We can start on this together? Right away?

I am your servant.

Amen.

A Morning Prayer

God, you have given me a new day.

I will make all I can of it.

I have air in my lungs.

I have food in my refrigerator.

There is coffee somewhere in the world, and I'm going to find it.

I work for the Creator of the universe.

What can mere humans do to me?

What can the weather do to me?

I am a servant of God.

(Lift up some things that have to be done today. Ask God to give you advice or help in dealing with them today.)

I will accomplish what I can.

I will forget about yesterday's problems.

I will learn yesterday's lessons.

I will prepare for tomorrow without worrying about it.

I am in this day.

I am in this moment.

God, you have given me a new day.

I will make all I can of it.

Amen.

An Evening Prayer

I have finished another day.

I haven't completed everything that was expected of me.

I haven't accomplished everything I'd hoped.

But then there is tomorrow.

I have spent another day as a servant of the Creator of the universe.

I go where I'm called (usually).

I do what I'm told (mostly).

You have a plan, right, God?

You have it all laid out in front of you, right?

I made it through this day.

The church did not burn down.

The universe did not implode.

All those horrible things I convinced myself would happen, did not.

This is a long-term thing, God.

Someday I will look back on these days and understand what your plan was.

In the meantime...

Give me patience.

Give me strength.

Give me rest; please give me rest.

(Take a moment to lift up to God those things that happened today that caused you stress or worry. Imagine loading all of these into a big black trash bag. Visualize God taking this bag from you and throwing it far away.)

Take my baggage, God.

Take my worries and my cares.

Let me feel your presence as I rest.

Give me peaceful dreams.

Wake me in the morning so this can all start again.

But for right now, just a little peace.

Amen.

A Prayer for the Middle of the Night during a Lock-In

They are giggling again, God.

Can you hear them?

They were supposed to be asleep hours ago.

Their parents are going to kill me.

That stain on the carpet isn't going to come out.

Why do they like lock-ins, God?

Don't they know what it does to my nerves?

I'm going to be so cranky in the morning.

Help me keep my sense of humor.

Send me just a little extra patience.

I'm going to crash and burn when I get back to my own bed.

We've been laughing and eating and talking and talking and talking.

Thank you for this moment of silence, God.

Thank you for this moment that is just you and me.

(Take a minute just to be silent. Listen to the room around you. Listen to what's outside. Relax and breathe deeply. Just be in the silence and let God's peace be in you.)

Thank you for this quiet, God.

Thank you for the students who actually want to be here.

Thank you also for the students who wish they were somewhere else.

Thank you for the parents who trust me with everything they hold most dear.

Thank you for the darkness.

Thank you for the breakfast food in the refrigerator.

Thank you for creating the coffee I'm going to be consuming great amounts of.

I am your servant.

Amen.

A Prayer When Nothing…No, Nothing…Is Going Right

It's not working, God.

Nothing—**not one thing**—worked out as it was supposed to.

They don't care.

They don't listen.

They ignore me.

I can't make the church board support me.

My budget is gone.

Everything I've touched today has turned to crap in my hands.

What am I supposed to do?

I love you, God.

I love Jesus.

Aren't you supposed to help me out with this?

Why do I feel like I'm alone?

Am I supposed to be learning something?

Is there a plan here that I'm missing?

Tell me what it is, and I'll do it.

Just get me through this day.

(Take a very deep breath.)

(Take another.)

(Take another.)

(Now take one more and mean it.)

(Put your finger in the page, close the book, and just sit for a minute.)

(Now, start again.)

(God is not your buddy—God is your GOD.)

(Say thank you for something.)

(Say thank you for something else.)

(Again.)

(One more.)

God, thank you for my life.

Thank you for this day.

There is much to learn.

I have such a narrow view. I see only one piece of the puzzle.

You see the completed picture.

I need strength, God.

I need encouragement.

Let me feel your hand on my shoulder.

Send your angels to come and stand around my chair.

Let me feel your presence.

Amen.

A Prayer When You Are Really, Really Pissed

God, right now, it's all I can do not to throw this book through the wall.

I feel like I could rip my door off its hinges.

I'm so angry I just want to turn into that big green guy and start throwing furniture around.

Do you know what's going on here, God?

Do you see what they are doing?

I thought I was the servant.

Why are you listening to them?

Why do they always win?

Why am I doing this job?

I could leave and go someplace and actually make money.

I want to break something.

I want to scream.

What do you want from me, God?

(Take a deep breath.)

(Now another.)

(Center yourself.)

(Breathe again.)

(Think about your students.)

(Think about the last really good mission trip.)

(Think about the time when a student did something special for you.)

(Remember that God knows exactly what is going on.)

(Breathe deeply.)

(Remember that God sees the big picture. You see just a piece of the puzzle.)

(Breathe deeply.)

(Focus on what's bothering you.)

{ 152 }   *(Breathe deeply.)*

God I'm putting this out in front of you.

You know all things—why am I angry with you?

I will do what you ask of me.

I will go where you send me.

Right now, give me just a little peace.

I am your servant, and you know exactly what you are doing.

Amen.

A Prayer When You Are Lost (Literally)

God, what did I miss?

How did we get here?

I really thought I knew what I was doing.

Why don't I get lost when I have time to get lost?

I can't tell east from west.

I can't tell up from a hole in the ground.

Is this what Moses felt like?

Just wandering...wandering...wandering...

I keep looking for signposts.

I keep looking for familiar street signs.

Who is the angel in charge of these things?

Am I all alone, God?

(Take a moment and relax.)

(Take a deep breath.)

(If you are driving, pull over.)

(If you have your students with you, ask them to be quiet and pray, too.)

(Stop looking around frantically and focus on the center of the steering wheel.)

(You are not lost.)

(You are here in the presence of God.)

(Nobody is that late.)

God, I'm going to start out again now.

Keep me sane.

Show me a landmark.

Give me an idea I'm headed in the right direction.

Show me what you brought me here to see.

Turn up the volume on whatever you want me to hear in this place.

Open my mind, soul, and heart to this experience.

I will learn from it.

Nobody stays lost.

I am on my way.

Amen.

A Prayer When You Are Lost (Figuratively)

God, I've got that spinning feeling going again.

I'm just running in circles.

I don't know where I'm going.

I don't know where I've been.

I don't know where I'm supposed to be.

I have so much to do, and I have no idea how to do it.

I've been doing this for a long time, and I don't know why or what for.

It's like I'm standing in the parking lot and can't find my car.

You'll drop me a sign, won't you?

A big flashing arrow that tells me what I'm supposed to do?

Can you do that for me, God?

(Take a deep breath.)

(Whisper to God what's making you feel this way.)

(Now shut up and listen.)

(God does not speak in hurricanes.)

(God speaks in small breezes.)

(Listen for a whisper. You might not hear it now.)

(God will let you know what to do.)

(God will give you the words to say.)

(God will plant your feet firmly so you don't feel lost.)

(God will give you a place to fully "be.")

David used to shout at you, God.

Moses used to complain.

And it seems like Paul *never* shut up.

You brought them all out of their emotional deserts, God.

You gave them all a sense of purpose and being.

Give me that same sense, God. I need it.

But I will wait.

Your time, not mine, right?

I will wait.

I am your servant.

Amen.

A Prayer for Your Spouse

God, there is a reason for the term "significant other."

I don't know where I would be without (her, him).

I don't think I could survive without (her, him).

(She, He) didn't bargain for this, God.

(She, He) didn't sign on for this kind of work.

This is my gig, not (hers, his).

Suddenly, our house is full of teenagers.

Suddenly, there are prank calls on our answering machine.

Suddenly, my cell phone never stops ringing.

I leave for weeks at a time.

I never have a weekend free.

It must seem like I live at the church.

(Think about your wedding.)

(God put two together and got one.)

(One plus one equals one—that's God math.)

(Thank God for your spouse.)

(Do it again.)

(Ask God to bless your marriage.)

(Ask God to help your board understand when you ask for a weekend off.)

(Ask God to help them understand that the youth program will not fall apart without you.)

I will make the time, God.

I will honor my vows.

I will show you how grateful I am for giving me (her, him).

I will make the time.

Amen.

Private Prayers for Youth Workers

A Prayer for Your Biggest Complainers

This is me on my knees, God.

See me?

I'm doing my best.

I'm loving my enemies.

Give me understanding, God.

Give me something I can do to let them know I'm capable.

Help me stop feeling like I'm worthless when they're around.

You put me here, God.

This is your design.

I will follow your lead on this.

What did I do to offend, God?

I'm doing your work.

It's like there's nothing I can do to make them happy.

Is there something missing from their own lives that makes them angry with me?

(Offer God your complainer(s) by name.)

(Pray that they receive God's grace.)

(Pray that God reaches down and heals whatever is broken inside them.)

(Pray that God lifts them up.)

(Ask God for strength to get through the moments you are with them.)

(Ask God for eyes and ears that can discover what you need to do to get along.)

(Ask God for patience and understanding.)

(Remember that Jesus' critics nailed him to a tree.)

God, love wins.

No matter what I do.

No matter what happens.

Love wins.

Amen.

A Five-Minute-Break Prayer

God, my door is closed.

My lights are off.

No one is going to bother me for the next five minutes.

It's just you and me.

I'm listening, God.

Speak. Say something.

I am your servant, and I'm listening.

Calm my nerves.

Give me strength.

Make me into the servant you want me to be.

I will go where you send me.

I will do what you tell me.

(Take a moment and sit in the silence.)

(Just sit there.)

(Don't say anything.)

Amen.

A Prayer When You Are Stuck in Traffic

God, I have places to be.

I'm your servant—you sent me.

Can't you make a path?

You parted the Red Sea.

Can't you help me out here?

I have this moment, God.

I have this here and now.

People are looking at me like I'm strange.

I'm talking to my God.

I'm also going to listen.

God, listen to me, then I'll listen to you.

(Tell God what's on your mind.)

(Don't make a list of complaints or wants.)

(Just talk to God as if you were writing a letter.)

(Talk to God as you'd talk to an old friend you haven't seen in a long time.)

(Then shut up and listen for a while.)

God, these moments, these times of just-you-and-me,

they restore my soul.

I will repeat them.

I will learn to listen without thinking of other things.

I will get better at this with practice, God.

We will talk.

We will become closer.

You are my God and my Maker.

Let me feel your presence.

Amen.

A Prayer When You've Been Fired

You saw that one coming, didn't you, God?

Was that me?

Am I not going where you want me to go?

Am I not doing what you want me to do?

Are your goals their goals?

Are your goals mine?

Are mine yours?

What exactly am I supposed to do now?

Any glimpse into that vast eternal plan of yours would be appreciated.

(Say this: God, I am your servant.)

(Say it out loud.)

(Say it again.)

(Say it over and over until you stop thinking about what you are going to do next.)

(Sat it over and over until you are ready to stop asking, "Why, God? Why?")

(Say it slowly.)

If I cannot serve you here, God, I will serve you someplace else.

I am the branch.

I am a beam of light from your flashlight.

I will go where I am told.

I will do what you want me to do.

I am a youth worker, and I work for the Creator of the universe.

What can puny humans do to me?

Amen.

A Prayer When You've Really Screwed Up

God, I am so royally screwed.

I could very well lose my job for this.

You didn't feel the need to jump in there at all?

You just let me dig that hole?

This was my fault, not yours.

I'm sure you're glad to know that, right?

This was huge, God.

There's a giant hole in the wall shaped like me, just like in the cartoons.

I just ran full speed, straight into it.

I don't know what's going to happen, God.

(Quietly offer a confession, just between you and God.)

(God knows what you did. He was there to watch, after all.)

(Confession is good for the soul.)

(Lighten your soul.)

(Tell God everything. Tell God your fears. Tell God your worries.)

(Unburden yourself.)

(When you are done, sit quietly and just "be.")

God, be with me.

This is the hardest part.

I have to make this right.

I have to face the music on this one.

I am your servant, and that won't change.

Even if I get canned.

I am yours.

If you still want me.

I am yours.

Amen.

A Prayer of Thanks

It doesn't get much better than this.

I work for the One who put the stars in the sky.

The One who put the tree by the stream.

The One who created all things.

I work for *that* Creator.

It's unbelievable God would choose me.

The Maker of all things thinks *I* am made for this.

Who am I to argue?

God says, "You—go."

I will go.

God made the grass green.

God made the sky blue.

God made mountains and ants.

God made angels and banana trees.

God made that spot where the water hits the beach.

God made that place where you can look out and see the whole world.

God made snow, rain, thunder, sunshine, colored leaves, new flowers.

God is good.

God is most definitely good.

(Think of your own list of good things from God.)

(God is in all things, so your list can include anything you want.)

(Now say thank you.)

(Think of some words that mean Good, Better, and Best.)

(Remember that God is all this and more.)

(Then tell God that.)

(Say it again.)

(And again.)

God, you are all these things.

You put me here.

I know there's a reason.

I will be your servant.

Amen.

A Prayer for Help Making a Hard Decision

God, I've thought about it a lot.

I've made lists of the pros and the cons.

I'm still at a loss.

If I don't make up my mind, someone else will make it up for me.

I need a little light here, God.

Not to light up the correct path,

but just a little illumination to help me decide.

God, give me wisdom.

Give me strength to live with whatever comes from my decision.

Give me the determination not to run backward if it all falls apart.

Turn my head so it faces forward.

Show me the path.

I will listen to your advice.

I will listen to those you have placed in my life to support and guide me.

I will listen with my heart.

(Think about your choices.)

(Think about the advice you've been given.)

(Think about who gave you that advice.)

(Open yourself to God's wisdom.)

(What is God putting in your heart?)

God, I will listen.

I will decide, even if your path is harder.

I will decide, even if your path may hurt.

I will do what I have to do.

Most of the time, I already know the answer, God.

Most of the time, I just need a kick in the butt to get me moving.

I will listen for your voice.

I will trust your words.

I will be your servant.

Amen.

{ 162 }

A Prayer When It's Time to Leave Your Comfort Zone

God, I've been going through the motions.

Not that it's all bad or anything.

The program is good. People like me. I like it here.

But, God, I'm bored out of my skull.

I can't keep doing it this way.

If I do, I'll become one of those people I complain about.

I will become beige.

I will become vanilla.

I can't do that to myself, God.

I need to shake things up, just for my own mental, emotional, and spiritual health.

This is like stage fright.

I need to let go of my fears and jump off the high board.

(What crazy ideas have been in your head lately? Tell God about them.)

(Who are the people most likely to make them happen?)

(What's the worst that could happen if you fail?)

(What's the best that could happen if you succeed?)

(Tell God about your fears. He's heard it all.)

(Tell God about your dreams. He put them there.)

(Ask God to clarify your vision and to give you the strength to take the first step.)

God, there is a freedom in trying new things.

I want to feel unchained.

I want to feel creative.

I don't like this rut.

Give me your hand, God.

Help me climb out.

Amen.

Lyrics and Notes for the Spirit, Draw Near CD

1. Come, Holy Spirit (4:10)

Jonny Baker and Jon Birch

Come, Holy Spirit, fill the hearts of
your people,
kindle in us the fire of your love

2. Spirit, Draw Near (4:12)

Adrian Riley

Spirit, draw near
life begins here
moving through me
come consume me

Christ, be here now
take my fear now
touch me, guide me
walk beside me

Spirit, draw near
life begins here
moving through me
come consume me

Moving, breathing
calming, healing
knowing, seeing
loving, feeling

Christ, be here now
take my fear now
touch me, guide me
walk beside me

I don't need proof
here i find love
one living word
Saviour, my Lord
Saviour, my Lord

God, be here now...

3. And Death Will Have No Dominion (4:18)

Jonny Baker and Jon Birch

Where O death is your sting?
Where is your victory?
Christ has plumbed the depths of
hell
And walked out with the key

This hope inspires me
This hope inspires me

In the midst of struggling
Recall the memory
Christ has triumphed over death
The final enemy

This hope inspires me
This hope inspires me

The dawning of a new age
A new humanity
Redemption of creation
Christ is the guarantee

This hope inspires me
This hope inspires me

4. When I Survey the Wondrous Cross (3:44)

Words Isaac Watts, 1707; Tune Rockingham

When I survey the wondrous cross
On which the Prince of glory died,
My richest gain I count but loss,
And pour contempt on all my
pride.

Forbid it, Lord, that I should boast,
Save in the death of Christ my
God!
All the vain things that charm me
most,
I sacrifice them to His blood.

See from His head, His hands, His feet,
Sorrow and love flow mingled down!
Did e'er such love and sorrow meet,
Or thorns compose so rich a crown?

Were the whole realm of nature mine,
That were an offering far too small:
Love so amazing, so divine,
Demands my soul, my life, my all.

5. Lay Your Burdens Down (5:28)

Iain Cotton

Lay your burdens down
The heavy load you carry with you
Lay your burdens down lay them down
Though they are hard times
You're going through
Responsibilities hang heavy on you
They're weighing you down
Lay your burdens down lay them down
Take a little time to rest in the Lord

Jesus says come to me
you who carry burdens
Jesus says come to me
you who carry burdens
Jesus he says come to me
and I will give you rest

Lay your burdens down
Lay your burdens down

6. Space and Time (5:36)

Jonny Baker and Jon Birch

Lay down burdens
breathe out stress
release pressure
shed some layers
lay down burdens
breathe out stress
release pressure
shed some layers

Take some space and time (x2)

Enter silence
breathe in life
embrace peace
gaze on Christ
enter silence
breathe in life
embrace peace
gaze on Christ

Take some space and time (x2)

You are loved
you are free
you are safe
you are clean
you are loved
you are free
you are safe
you are clean

7. Ps 33 (2:14)

Stray

When the big wave hits
When the crash comes
Let me find you, God
My hiding place
Protection
Protection in troubles
Surround me

{ 167 }

Surround me with songs
Surround me with songs of deliverance

8. Love Theme (3:20)

Stray
(instrumental)

9. God Above (3:49)

Andy Thornton

God above
God below
God within
God we long for

10. The Lord's My Shepherd (3:21)

Words Scottish Psalter, 1650; Tune Crimmond (Jessie S Irvine, 1872)

The Lord's My Shepherd, I'll not
want
He makes me down to lie
In pastures green; He leadeth me
The quiet waters by.

My soul He doth restore again;
And me to walk doth make
Within the paths of righteousness,
Even for His own Name's sake.

Yea, though I walk in death's dark
vale,
Yet will I fear no ill;
For Thou art with me; and Thy rod
And staff my comfort still.

My table Thou hast furnishèd
In presence of my foes;
My head Thou dost with oil anoint,
And my cup overflows.

Goodness and mercy all my life
Shall surely follow me;
And in God's house forevermore
My dwelling place shall be.

11. Table of Christ (6:04)

Jonny Baker and Jon Birch

All are invited, all are included
All are made welcome, none are
excluded
This is the table of Christ
Come if you're young
Come if you're old
Come if you're broken
Come if you're whole
Come if you're weary
of the trials of life
This is the table of Christ

This is the table of Christ (x2)

Jesus the host washes your feet
Makes you his guest and lays on a
feast
This is the table of Christ
Come if you're rich
Come if you're poor
Come if the church
stops you at the door
Come and eat bread
Come and drink wine
This is the table of Christ

This is the table of Christ (x2)

Eat and remember Jesus the One
who gave up his life so you could
belong
This is the table of Christ
Come if you're thirsty
Come and be filled
Come and be clean
Come and be healed
Come and be held

in the presence of God
This is the table of Christ

12. Hope (4:10)

Jonny Baker and Jon Birch

When the night is at its darkest
Appears the morning star
A promise of the coming dawn
Dreamers of the future
living against the odds
Bring newness to a weary land

Seeds of hope
Seeds of hope
Dare to sow seeds of hope

13. Stars (6:40)

Jonny Baker and Jon Birch
(instrumental)